THE AUTHOR

Pierluigi Romeo di Colloredo Mels was born in Rome in 1966.
Archaeologist and military historian, he is the author of numerous works on the history of the two world wars and the Italian interwar conflicts, Ethiopia and Spain, and of the units of the MVSN. Among his latest works, *Camicia Nera! Storia delle unità combattenti della Milizia Volontaria Sicurezza Nazionale dalle origini al 25 luglio, Südfront. Il Feldmaresciallo Albert Kesselring nella campagna d'Italia 1943- 1945; Da Sidi el Barrani a Beda Fomm 1940- 1941; Per vincere ci vogliono i leoni... I fronti dimenticati delle camicie nere, 1939- 1940; Controguerriglia! La 2a Armata italiana e l'occupazione dei Balcani 1941- 1943; Confine orientale. Italiani e slavi sull'Amarissimo dal Risorgimento all'esodo; Giugno 1940. La battaglia delle Alpi.* In the Witness to War Series he has published Italian Black Shirts on Eastern Fron, 1941- 1943 (WtW EN 17).
Colloredo is also editor of *Storia Rivista* and collaborates with the magazines *Nova Historica, Storia in Rete, Ritterkreuz, Fronti di guerra* and *Il Primato Nazionale*.

PUBLISHING'S NOTES

None of unpublished images or text of our book may be reproduced in any format without the expressed written permission of Luca Cristini Editore (already Soldiershop.com) when not indi-cate as marked with license creative commons 3.0 or 4.0. Luca Cristini Editore has made every reasonable effort to locate, contact and acknowledge rights holders and to correctly apply terms and conditions to Content. Every effort has been made to trace the copyright of all the photo-graphs. If there are unintentional omissions, please contact the publisher in writing at: in-fo@soldiershop.com, who will correct all subsequent editions.
Our trademark: Luca Cristini Editore@, and the names of our series & brand: Soldiershop, Wit-ness to war, Museum book, Bookmoon, Soldiers&Weapons, Battlefield, War in colour, Histori-cal Biographies, Darwin's view, Fabula, Altrastoria, Italia Storica Ebook, Witness To History, Soldiers, Weapons & Uniforms, Storia etc. are herein @ by Luca Cristini Editore.

LICENSES COMMONS

This book may utilize part of material marked with license creative commons 3.0 or 4.0 (CC BY 4.0),(CC BY-ND 4.0), (CC BY-SA 4.0) or (CC0 1.0). We give appropriate attribution credit and indicate if change were made in the acknowledgments field. Our WTW books series utilize only fonts licensed under the SIL Open Font License or other free use license.

For a complete list of Soldiershop titles please contact Luca Cristini Editore on our website: www.soldiershop.com or www.cristinieditore.com. E-mail: info@soldiershop.com

Title: **WHITE DEVILS! "MONTE CERVINO" ALPINE SKI BATTALION 1941- 1943**
Code.: **WTW-019 EN** By Pierluigi Romeo di Colloredo Mels
ISBN CODE: 978-88-93276801 November 2020 (ebook ISBN 9788893276818)
Language: English Nr. di immagini: 121 dimensione: 177,8x254mm Cover & Art Design: Luca S. Cristini
WITNESS TO WAR (SOLDIERSHOP) is a trademark of Luca Cristini Editore, via Orio, 35/4 - 24050 Zanica (BG) ITALY.

WITNESS TO WAR

WHITE DEVILS! "MONTE CERVINO" ALPINE SKI BATTALION, 1941- 1943

PHOTOS & IMAGES FROM WORLD WARTIME ARCHIVES

PIERLUIGI ROMEO DI COLLOREDO MELS

BOOKS TO COLLECT

SUMMARY

Foreword, by Leutenant Colonel Giulio Lepore, Director, *Museo Nazionale Storico degli Alpini*

The creation of *Monte Cervino* Ski Battalion and its fight on the Greek Front

The reconstitution of the *Monte Cervino* Ski Battalion and its dispatch to the Eastern Front.

Monte Cervino operational employ on the Eastern Front. From the First Defensive Battle of the Don to the retreat (August 1942- January 1943)

Monte Cervino today

Photos

Bibliography

THIS WORK IS PUBLISHED WITH THE KIND COLLABORATION OF THE *MUSEO STORICO NAZIONALE DEGLI ALPINI*

www.museonazionalealpini.it

FOREWORD, BY LEUTENANT COLONEL GIULIO LEPORE, DIRECTOR OF *MUSEO NAZIONALE STORICO DEGLI ALPINI*

Monte Cervino, Matterhorn.

For those who love the mountains, Monte *Cervino* (or Matterhorn) is the name of an extraordinary peak, its imposing 4478 meters soar majestically and dominate the other peaks, this name arouses respect and admiration.

In the history of the Alpini, the name Monte *Cervino* is legend, it was given to the Battalion of troops chosen in the chosen body, it is synonymous with heroism, firmness, sacrifice and duty. The origin of the *Monte Cervino* Battalion has its roots in the evolution of the Corps, forged by the needs imposed by the war and by the specific operating environment in which the Alpine troops have always had to operate.

There are two decisive aspects in the genesis and formation of the *Monte Cervino* Battalion.

The first fundamental element that characterized the Monte *Cervino* Battalion is the use of skiing. In 1902, at the dawn of the use of skiing in the Alpine departments, men were trained to use the new means: at first, there were few for company (3rd Skiers co.), but over time the ski platoons were created that had reconnaissance tasks ; later, during the First World War, the skier companies formed by three platoons were born, companies that were then grouped two by two into the different battalions. Once the needs dictated by the conflict ended, these battalions were dissolved: the experience gained in the field confirmed the effectiveness of both the new vehicle and these specialized units.

The second element included in the DNA of the *Monte Cervino* Battalion is linked to Fiamme Verdi and that is, to those assault units that were born and operated between '17 and '18: the companies of *Fiamme Verdi* and the assault units entirely composed of Alpini: the 3rd *Reparto d'Assalto*, the 29th *Reparto d'Assalto* and the 52nd *Reparto d'Assalto*.

The reckless intelligence and reconnaissance operation is part of the same picture, following the daring air launch behind the enemy lines of Lieutenant Pier Arrigo Barnaba (Golden Medal for military bravery) with Lieutenant Alessandro Tandura (also Golden Metal for bravery) in 1818.

These two peculiarities are substantial in the essence of the *Cervino*, they arise from the need for mountain warfare, a special war that, at the time, had determined the very birth of the Corps; the operations that the Alpine troops should have conducted, precisely due to the constraints imposed by the mountain environment, had to be achieved with the techniques of guerrilla warfare, operating in small isolated groups: this doctrine in conducting the operations was the main characteristic that distinguished the Alpini in both conflicts. *Monte Cervino*, exalted this peculiarity, of being used in small autonomous nuclei capable of particular and extremely daring operations.

Between the two World Wars, with the birth of regimental competitions, the awareness of having to train the staff and the birth of the Alpine Military School, the right emphasis was also placed on the use of skiing. After the successful use of the skiers and assault units (the Btg. *Duca degli Abruzzi*, Autonomous Group. *Monte Bianco* with the *Arditi Alpieri* Department) in the French countryside, two ski battalions were formed, *Monte Cervino* and *Monte Rosa* with men chosen from the Alpine School and the Alpini Regiments: they were both sent to Albania at the beginning of '41 and were then dissolved in May at the end of the war with Greece.

The Matterhorn was reconstituted in October of 1941 by Lt. Col. D'Adda to be sent to fight in Russia first with the C.S.I.R and then in the ARMIR. The Alpine troops, all volunteers, had to know how to ski and be willing to do anything.

In Russia the legend of the *Satanas Bieli* (the white devils as the *Cervinotti* were called by the enemy) was born; chosen soldiers, men of the impossible, 600 lions who faced all difficulties and battles with incredible courage: the three Golden medals for military bravery, 42 Silver medals, 68 Bronze medals, 81 War crosses, most of which are attributed to deaths; but as evidence of their value, sacrifice and contempt for danger, only remain seventy-five survivors who returned to their homeland.

After the war, a study was conducted by Colonel Scotti, of the Alpine Troops, to evaluate the effectiveness of the use of parachutes in the mountains, so on September 1st, 1952 the 1st Platoon Alpini Paratroopers was born in the *Tridentina* Alpine Brigade staff; Then, in 1953, the platoons in staff of the other Alpine Brigades will follow: units always constituted on a voluntary basis.

On April 1st, 1964, in order to make the use of platoons organic and under a single command, they were reunited in Bolzano, forming the *Compagnia Alpini Paracadutisti, Alpini Paratrooper Alpine Company*.

The Alpini Paratroopers Company, in 1990, finally had the honor of inheriting the name of "Monte *Cervino*".

In July 1996 the "Monte *Cervino*" Parachute Alpini Company was elevated to the rank of battalion, with the same name.

The peculiarity and the actual capabilities of the battalion, linked to the new need to create a pool of special forces within the Army, despite the reductive reform in progress of the Armed Force which provided for the organic reduction of units, mean that in September 2004, it is raised to the rank of Regiment, acquiring the war flag and the name of the glorious 4th Alpine Regiment.

The evolution of these chosen soldiers, heirs of the tradition of the Matterhorn is unstoppable, and with the achievement by the personnel of the Ranger operator qualification, the 4th Alpine Parachute Regiment becomes a unit of Special Forces of the Italian Army. I had the honor and privilege of serving both in the Monte *Cervino* Battalion and in the 4th Alpine Parachute Regiment, from the rank of Junior Leutnant to that of Leutnant Colonel.; I had the privilege of commanding the 2nd Alpini Paratroopers Company and baptizing it *"Black Angels"*, I won the rank of Ranger, I loved and cursed a unique department in the world, as the men who belong to *Cervino* are unique: beyond of technology, specialization and training, what accompanies us and will always guide us is the unshakable awareness of who we are today and the duty to always be worthy of the name we bear, in honor of those who preceded us.

Leutenant Colonel Giulio Lepore,
Director, *Museo Nazionale Storico degli Alpini*

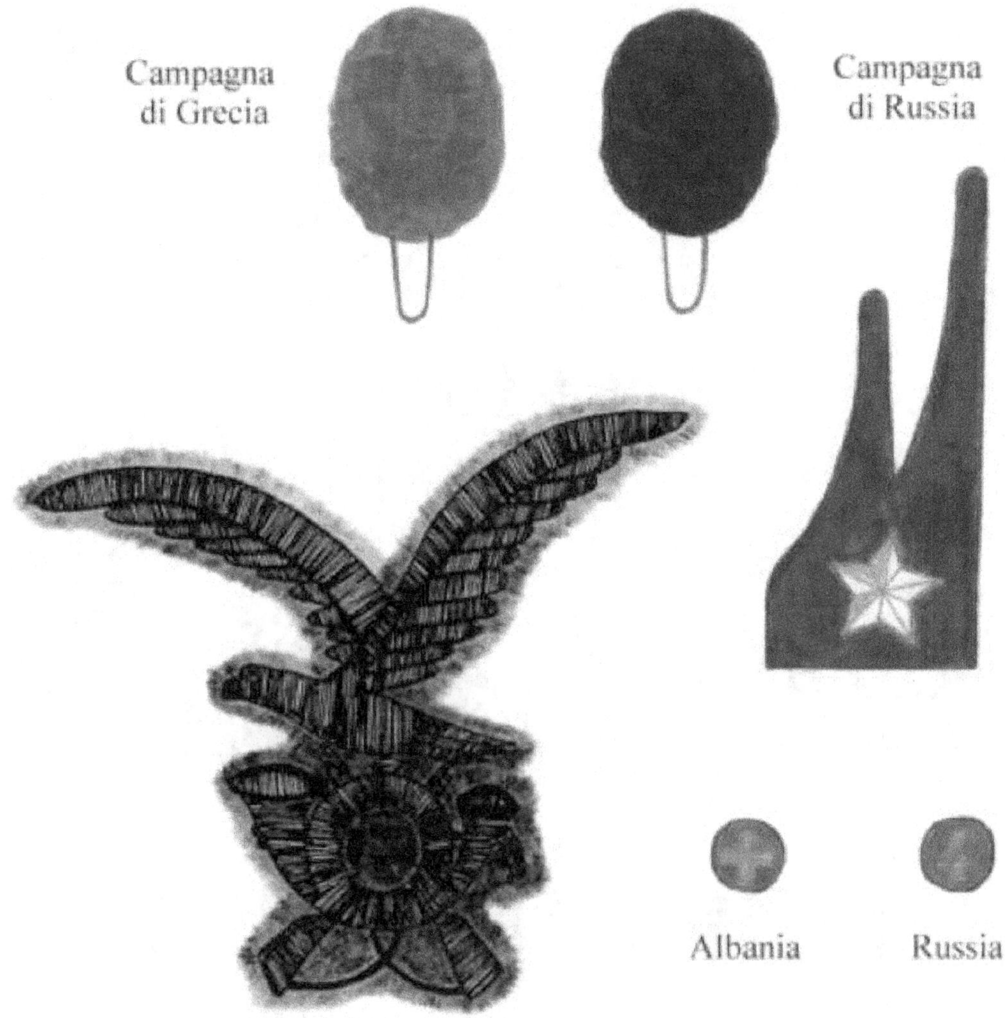

▲ Cap eagle and green flames of the Battalion Monte Cervino. The tassel was blue (Alpine School of Aosta) in Greece, red in Russia.

▼ Badge of the Skiers Battalion Monte Cervino.

▲ Postcard of the *Duke of Abruzzi* battalion. The postcard is by the painter Tafuri.

▼ Medal of the *Duke of Abruzzi* battalion.

THE CREATION OF THE *MONTE CERVINO* SKI BATTALION AND ITS FIGHT ON THE GREEK FRONT

In June 1940, at the outbreak of the war against France, the Aosta Alpine Training Military School (Scuola Alpina di Aosta) had put in line, to be employed on the western front, a Battalion made up of highly selected personnel, the *Duca degli Abruzzi* Battalion, which ceased the emergency on the Alpine front was dissolved on the very day the Italian invasion of Greece began, October 28, 1940.

The name of the Battalion already indicated the very high specialization. Luigi of Savoy Aosta, Duke of the Abruzzi, son of Amedeo di Savoy king of Spain, admiral of Squadra, Mountaineer, Arctic explorer, had been one of the pioneers of high altitude mountaineering, climbing first, in addition to numerous Alpine peaks, the peaks of Mount St Elias (1897: 5.489m, the highest mountain in North America) and of Mount Ruwenzori (1906: 5.109m .Margherita Peak, so named in honor of the Queen of Italy, and Alexandra), up to then never reached by man; made expeditions to Alaska, North Pole (1899-1900, on the Polar Star the Duke of Abruzzi reached the maximum Arctic latitude of 86° 33 '49 "until then reached by man), Somalia and the Karakorum where he climbed the slopes of K2 (1909: without reaching the top, conquered only in 1954, he conquered the world altitude record), first European, and circumnavigated the globe three times. In the Great War the Duke commanded the Italian fleet in the Adriatic Sea.

Dedicated to agricultural colonization, he founded a model village in Somalia, in Johar (Villaggio *Duca degli Abruzzi*) where he was buried until his tomb was destroyed and the remains were dispersed by Islamic militias in 2006.

After the dissolution order, the counterorder arrived in December: it was necessary to set up a Battalion made up of selected soldiers, mountain guides and ski instructors, without marriage ties, to be sent to Albania as soon as possible.

This elite unit was formed with personnel from the Alpine Military Training School of Aosta and by men of the 4th Alpini Regiment recruited in the Piedmontese mountains, and was named as a glorious Battalion of the Great War, *Mount Cervino*, constituted in 1915 within the 4th Regiment and disbanded in 1919, of which it received the gagliardetto (pennant[1]) and traditions, including the Silver medal for military bravery obtained for the mountain fights in WW1:

> The *Cervino* Battalion under a firestorm, exhausted in numbers but not in strength, fiercely resisted in serious situation to overwhelming enemy forces, covering itself with glory, at the price of pure blood, for the superhuman heroic passion of its Alpini who always gave shining example of the highest spirit of sacrifice.
>
> — Melette, November 17-26th,1917; M. Bisorte, May 1916; Bodrez, May 15-18th, 1917; Vodice, May 26-30th, 1917; M. Fior, December 4th, 1917.

---
[1] Italian Battalions have no war flag

All the men of the newly formed Battalion were, as mentioned, ski instructors and alpine guides, what made the unity the best among the mountain troops of the various parties in conflict in terms of personnel selection and training; celibacy was among the various requisites for enlistment. The Battalion was also characterized by the war cry: *Pista! (Stay away!)* instead of the traditional battle cry *Savoia!* or *Avanti Alpini! Forward Alpini!* The tassel (*nappina*) on the Alpine hat was blue like that of the Aosta School.

Like other units sent in a hurry from the motherland, the *Cervino* served as a tap-pabuchi to close the holes created by the continuous Greek offensive actions.

Having landed in Durres on 18th January, the Alpini had passed directly from the ship to the trucks that had brought them to Tepeleni, from which, on foot, they had immediately reached the position assigned on Mali Trebeshines, in Dragoti.

On January 21st, 1941, the *Cervino* had the first deaths on the Greek front, hit by a mortar fire from the Greek lines.

The Battalion had 340 men on two companies, plus a commanding platoon.

The position assigned to the *Cervino* was a position then unguarded, at the junction of two large units. The enemy's effort was unleashed against this weak point and for three days the *Cervino* fought without receiving food rations. Here is the account of a surviving officer, Lieutenant Cossard:

> We did not have time to get to know our men: when we tried to re-assume the facts in writing, it was only exceptionally possible to give a name to the Alpine that we had seen falling next to us.

January 23rd and 24th the two companies of the Battalion, fighting separately, suffered 14 men dead, 37 wounded and 21 missing.

In the first days the companies were immediately deprived of their commanders: the two commanders, the captains Brillarelli and Mautino, were killed; Adjutant Astorri, who had wanted to go out with a patrol, was also killed. The Battalion did not receive alternations, rest shifts, the rations rarely managed to get hot on the front line, when it arrived: as a post-war chronicle writes,

> For a whole month his battle lasted, fought by platoons and by squads, in front of the enemy or behind him aggregated now at this time to that infantry Division, often without connections, so that the more serious decisions sometimes took the corporals. The whole Eleventh Army soon met those wonderful soldiers with blue tassels, the "*Cervinotti*" who never went to rest and who only left Albania when they were sixty, with Commander Anelli and some wounded officers in the hospital and the others buried in the Battalion's graveyard.

The losses among the officers were such that for some days the command of the Battalion was held by two second lieutenants.

Another time a non-commissioned officer, Giacomo Chiara, a Piedmontese from Alagna Sesia, found himself the highest ranking officer of Monte *Cervino* Battalion while the Greek euvzones attacked the remains of the Battalion after a very hard artillery fire.

Chiara remained crouched in the shelter until the moment when the enemy started to attack; when he heard the high cry of the Greeks, he jumped to the highest point of the trench, standing tall, colossal, with the machine gun braced like a child's rifle, and immediately began to shoot and shoot, changing the weapon, always erect in all his two meters in the middle of the bullets, alone in front of the enemy, calm, precise, invulnerable. He only descended when the enemy turned back, and all the Alpini jumped on him laughing and crying to touch him; he was really unharmed, not a scratch, he just wanted to drink, earning the reputation of being lucky and carrying good things: when the survivors returned to Aosta, everyone wanted to see and touch Chiara, who had been promoted to battle adjutant; when he entered a dormitory of recruits, everyone stood at attention and when he went out they followed him as in procession.

A month after his arrival in Albania, the *Cervino* had practically ceased to exist as an organic department; he had fought only one, continuous battle, but without being able to be used for the purposes for which it was created: infiltrations, hand strikes, or being able to use skis due to the particular climatic conditions that alternated seamlessly snow and mud.

On March 5th what remained of the Battalion was sent to Mali Scindeli, where it remained until April 10th, reducing itself to the strength of a platoon.

Losses on the Greek front were 14 of 19 dead or wounded officers (including eight replacements), 8 of 13 dead or wounded non-commissioned officers, and 153 of 208 Alpini killed or wounded.

The Battalion was awarded the Silver Medal for military bravery with the following motivation:

> For three months and in a particularly delicate situation, with an admirable spirit of sacrifice and unwavering faith, overcoming the rigors of a harsh winter, he maintained possession of a large high mountain front, bitterly contested by overwhelming forces. Present everywhere, daring in the blizzard of the mountains and in the blizzards of fire, with indomitable valor he opposed tenacious resistance, crushing the enemy's impetus in bloody attacks and swooping lightly on the opponent's flanks and back, breaking the formations. Thus he showed that courage is worth more than numbers and weapons.
>
> *Greek Front, January 10th, 1941 - April 23rd, 1941.*

▲ The "Military Patrol" of the Alpine School of Aosta won the Biathlon demonstration race at the 1936 Olympics in Garmisch. The race took place on a course of 25 km with 600 meters of altitude difference. The Italian patrol, composed as per regulations by one officer, one NCO and two soldiers, completed the course in 2h 28' and 35" beating Finland, Sweden and Austria in order. The Duke of Abruzzi battalion was trained with this type of personnel, all mountain guides and ski instructors; note the characteristic white hemp equipment.

▼ Lt. Col. D'Adda (left) commander of 'Monte Cervino' with Capt. Giuseppe Lamberti.

▲ Patrol of the Matterhorn Battalion on Mali Trebescines in the winter of 1941. Grey-green leather giberne are still in use.

▼ Greek front. Alpine skiers of the "Matterhorn" marching in the mountains in winter 1941.

▲ Patrol of Mount Cervino on Mali Trebescines in the winter of 1941.

▼ An Alpine ski patrol marching on Mali Trebescines in the winter of 1941. The musket is the 91/38 long; later it was replaced by the 91/38 TS short with folding bayonet.

▲ Alpini of the Cervino in action on Mali Trebescines.

▼ Alpine skiers marching in the snow in winter 1941.

▲ A patrol of Matterhorn skiers in exploration.

▼ Skiers of Monte Cervino on Mali Trebescines, 1941.

▲ Lieutenant Colonel Mario D'Adda, commander of the battalion in Russia.

▲ The 80th Armi d'Accompagnamento company.

▼ The company deployed before departure for the Russian front.

▲The Prince of Piedmont Umberto di Savoia meets the Alpini of Monte Cervino about to leave for the Russian front. Next to Umberto is Commander D'Adda.

▼ Brenner Pass, 1941. Two Alpini of the "Monte Cervino". Note the uniform with the long skier's trousers and the white cloth cloakroom 32 (courtesy of the National Historical Alpine Museum).

▲ The Alpino Osvaldo Bartolomei of the 80th AA Company photographed in Russia in the summer of 1941. He wears the typical summer outfit of Monte Cervino with white hemp buffets with four giberas, long ski trousers and boots with vibram soles.

THE RECONSTITUTION OF THE *MONTE CERVINO* SKI BATTALION AND ITS DISPATCH TO THE EASTERN FRONT (1941- 1942)

In spring, Major Salomone, the new commander of the Battalion, brought back sixty men to Italy, including the non-commissioned officer Maltempi from Domodossola, mutilated in his leg; and the medical lieutenant Lincio, also wounded, but recovered before he fell into the hands of the enemy.

The Monte Cervino Battalion was officially dissolved at the end of the campaign against Greece, but in November 1941 the order came to reconstitute it in view of employment on the Russian Front. Among the first to show up was the newly recovered medical lieutenant Lincio, another doctor friend of his, lieutenant Enrico Reginato wanted to follow him but had a sick foot. In order not to go to the hospital he operated himself, on the train. So it was that the medical lieutenant Enrico Reginato left for the eastern front with one finger less, to remain there for twelve years, a prisoner of the Soviet regime, in spite of international law and in appalling conditions, for its irreducible anti-communism.

Reginato was awarded the Golden Medal for Military Bravery:

> Medical officer of an Alpini Battalion already distinguished for attachment to duty and disregard of danger on the battlefield, for over eleven years of imprisonment he was, as a doctor, apostle of his humanitarian mission and, as an officer, shining example of proud character, moral uprightness, dedication to the distant homeland and to the duty of a soldier. Indifferent to the sacrifice of his own life, he worked tirelessly in the care of those affected by dangerous epidemic forms until he himself was seriously infected. With makeshift means that did not offer him the most elementary precautionary measures, he did not hesitate to face the danger of the most serious infections, in order to operate and alleviate the suffering of the sick and wounded entrusted to his care. Subjected, for his patriotic faith and attachment to duty, first to the most tempting flattery and, immediately after, to torture, threats and harsh punishments, he never failed to the dignity and nobility of his feelings of boundless altruism, very high love of country, incorruptible righteousness, sense of duty.
>
> Russia, 1942-1954.

For the reconstitution of the Monte Cervino Battalion, 30 volunteer Skiers were requested from each Alpini Regiment, to be equipped and armed with new criteria.

The planned staff was structured on Command and two companies with a regional structure, the 1st with Ligurians and Piedmontese men and the 2nd with Lombard and Venetians, formed by a command team and 3 platoons, each with 2 machine gun teams and one of fusiliers.

In total, the staff consisted of 14 officers, 25 non-commissioned officers and 281 Alpini, with 12 submachine guns, 20 Beretta machine guns (6 per company and 8 in command, for officers and foremen) but without the Breda 37 machine guns provided.

Battalion commander was Lieutenant Colonel Mario D'Adda, a veteran of the Great War who as a second lieutenant found himself commanding the remains of a Battalion that descended from Ortigara, receiving a reproach because the uniforms were in disorder: among thousands of volunteers who applied to enter the Cervino, D'Adda chose them one by one, according to the old rule: all ski instructors or alpine guides, all celibate.

D'Adda requested and obtained special equipment, designed specifically for fighting in the high mountains, so much so that the Alpine Skiers were perhaps the best equipped Axis troops for the harsh temperatures on the Russian front in 1942.

Over the ordinary gray-green uniform, worn with the turtleneck sweater instead of the shirt, the Skiers wore a windbreaker and loose-fitting white waterproof overtrousers.

Unlike the other Alpine departments, in the Cervino gray-green uniforms were not worn the gray-green short pants with mollettier bands, but the long skier's ones. Sleeveless sheepskin jackets were also distributed to be worn over the windbreaker as additional protection from the cold.

The Alpini of Monte Cervino were supplied with balaclavas and white or gray-green wool gloves, white woolen caps to possibly wear under the helmet which is the usual M33, painted in gray-green and with feather and tassel, covered in winter with a with e camouflage cloth; the feathers worn on caps and helmets were black for militaries, brown for non-commissioned officers and junior officers and white for senior officers; the tassels were red for the troops and non-commissioned officers, and gilt bronze for the officers.

On their feet the Cervinotti wore woolen socks and ski boots with special Vibram rubber soles, perfectly insulating.

Instead of the usual italian gray-green leather jackets, the Cervino was supplied with special four-pocket white canvas jackets; in addition to these supplied there were the haversack and gas mask bags made of canvas model 35 and the two-liter water bottle for alpine troops covered with gray-green cloth. The skis were built in steel laminated ash, in three different sizes; the average one was 210 cm long, 72-75 mm wide with a fairly relevant thickness and reinforced tail; the guide groove and lamination were obtained in the thickness. From the middle of the skis forward, from 2 cm forward to the stirrup, a 30 cm long strip of linoleum or aluminum was fixed which prevented the snow from getting between the ski and the foot. The bindings with pivot lever were 68-75 mm wide with a soft iron stirrup fitted with a longitudinal I-window and an inner face covered in leather, which fit into a split in the middle of the ski.

The weapons supplied were the 91/38 musket for special weapons with foldable or unstable bayonet, Beretta M38 machinegun (MAB 38), Beretta M34 and M35 8mm pistols, the daring dagger, OTO and Breda hand grenades and, as team support weapon, the Breda M30 6.5mm light machine gun. In addition to these Italian-made weapons, on the Russian front, weapons from other armies in the field were also used whenever possible, in particular the MP40 sub-pistol, the 9mm Luger pistol, the German-made stielhandgrenade, much more effective than the OTO. and the Soviet PPSh-40 submachine gun of war booty.

The Cervino had two companies of Skiers, to which was added the 80th company A.A. (accompanying weapons); his strength reached six hundred men. Instead of Finland, the destination was the Don plain. In this regard, it must be said that this was due to the contingent needs due to the intensification of Soviet offensive activities.

Meanwhile, given the deteriorating situation in the U.S.S.R. (the Germans had been pushed back from Moscow and Leningrad, and Timoshenko had created a vast bridgehead in Isjum) Hitler asked Mussolini to send other troops, especially the Alpine Divisions, to be employed in the Caucasus, also driven by the brilliant results of the CSIR.

The first German request for other Italian troops dates back to January 1, 1942, when Hitler sent a message to the il Duce in which he praised the combativeness of the Italians, adding that a new dispatch of troops was desirable, if possible already during the winter, which, however, was not deemed possible by the Italian General Staff, which sent, pending the rest, which would arrive in Russia in the spring-summer, only one Alpini unit: the Monte Cervino Battalion, destined to operate on the Don.

The use of the Alpini in the plains has aroused controversy, not always well founded. We recall that - apart from the fact that Germans, Romanians and Hungarians normally employed mountain troops in the plains - the Alpine Army Corps had been destined to be employed in the Caucasus, and was diverted to the Don as a matter of urgency due to the Soviet offensive of August 1942. Von General Erno von Rintelen testifies that when the OKW asked Rome for authorization to use the Alpini in the Caucasus,

> Mussolini expressed to me his great satisfaction for such a replacement by his Alpini, who as mountain troops were neither armed nor trained for a war on the plains.

The Battalion left for the front after being reviewed by Umberto di Savoia, Prince of Piedmont, who at first had been hypothesized as commander of the Italian army in Russia. As the German military attaché in Rome Enno von Rintelen recalls, General Cavallero asked him to probe the opinion of the OKW regarding the command to Umberto, but Hitler strongly opposed, as Keitel wrote to gen. Reintelen.

The thing was then dropped, and General Italo Gariboldi, who had already collaborated with the Germans in Libya in 1941, was chosen for the command.

Morale was high, and relations with allies were excellent.

Alpine Claudio Isoardi, of the Cervino Battalion, writes:

> Germany, 21st January 1942,
>
> We will win! (...) The camaraderie of our allies is spontaneous and very nice their sympathy for us Alpini, they call us Alpiniegher [sic for Alpenjaeger], our Italian brothers (...).

The Battalion's journey to Ukraine lasted about a month, from January 13th to February 18th, 1942. The unit was deployed in the Dnepropetrovsk area, and soon moved to the front line in the sector of General Messe's 35th Army Corps.

The Battalion's employ on the Russian front lasted exactly twelve months: the first fight took place on 24th March 1942 at -32° below zero on the Ploski front (Olovatka).

By mistake, the 1st company was invited into an open space between two strong Soviet positions, and moreover, due to the temperature of -32, the Breda M30 machine guns stopped, causing no support fire; in the end, the 2nd company managed to get the 1st company out of the way, with the loss of six fallen, about 20 injured and 30 frozen. This reverse, albeit of little importance, demonstrated the need for greater firepower, and it was decided to equip the Battalion with an Heavy Weapons Company (Compagnia Armi d'Accompagnamento, AA), the 80th, with two 81mm mortar platoons, each with four pieces, two machine gun platoons, two antitank platoons, each with two 47/32 guns and four tow tractors.

In one year the Cervino was destined to operate where necessary, almost always moving by ordinary route, that is, moving on foot. Remember the Alpine Osvaldo Bartolomei, of the 80th AA company, the last survivor of the Battalion still alive:

> Later we went on. Endless fields of sunflowers.
>
> The impression was that the Russians were withdrawing on purpose, leaving aggressive rearguards to slow the advance of the opposing troops. They were the feelings of twenty-year-old boys, it's not that we knew much.
>
> We knew that the Soviet general in command of the opposing troops in our sector was Tymoshenko. We walked ... once, during these marches, my friend Bizzarri showed me a note found in a box containing musket magazines. It belonged to a girl from our area, probably employed - at the S.M.I. - to the packaging department I mentioned at the beginning: encouraging words for us soldiers were written on the ticket. Returning to our marches.
>
> (...) Since there were not enough means of transport, one day the 1st Company moved; the next day the 1st remained stationary and was joined by the 2nd Company.
>
> In any case, despite the stretches traveled aboard the trucks, the kilometers on foot were many. I think that the Heavy Weapons Company, having the guns and mortars, had its own means to move.

▲ Rikowo railway station in 1942. The Matterhorn Battalion arrived there on March 2nd, 1942 to reinforce the Turin division.

▲ Matterhorn car column towards the front.

▼ Column of Soviet prisoners, summer 1942.

▲ The 80th AA company on the march with 47/32 anti-tank parts in action at Izjum in summer 1942.

▼ A 47/32 counter-truck cannon dragged by the servants.

▲ The hand-drawn pieces are about to arrive at the front line.

▼ Close-up of a 47/32 cannon.

▲ The 80th cp AA gunners pull the pieces. Note the light equipment.

▼ The gunners of the 80th AA reach the edge of the "balka".

▲ The 47/32 cannons are positioned in the front line.

▼ 47/32 counter-carton cannon ready to fire...

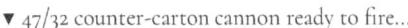

▲ The cannon opens fire on the Soviets.

▼ The 47/32 pieces hit the Soviet positions.

▲ The Alpini observe the fire on the Soviet lines before the attack (courtesy of the National Historical Alpine Museum).

▼ Two radio sets from the company Commando.

MONTE CERVINO OPERATIONAL EMPLOY ON THE EASTERN FRONT. FROM THE FIRST DEFENSIVE BATTLE OF THE DON TO THE RETREAT (AUGUST 1942- JANUARY 1943)

Monte Cervino was used according to the circumstances as independent unit, with the Julia, with German Divisions, with the *Barbò* Horsegroup; in some cases it operated as a whole, as a Battalion, or divided into dozens of patrols.

Several Skiers were awarded with Iron Crosses of Second Class (EK 2. kl.); also the German bulletin mentioned the *Cervino* Battalion.

On May 18th, 1942, the Battalion received orders to occupy the village of Klinowy during the battle of Izjum. The village was occupied when two Regiments of Soviet riflemen attacked the *Cervino* in the village with the intention of reoccupying Klinowy and then overwhelming the starting line of the Battalion.

D'Adda made the Battalion fall back to a point set by him, stopped the sovi-ethics before the Italian line and two days later returned to the attack and resumed the village.

The Soviet reaction provoked by the attack of the Alpini was in turn countered by the artillery fire of the Turin Division.

The attack of the *Monte Cervino* overwhelmed the Soviet advanced lines and provoked the influx of reinforcements, easing the Soviet pressure on Izjum, where the *Bersaglieri* of the XVIII Battalion of the 3rd *Celere* Division fought.

The Alpini had 15 dead and 40 wounded.

Not an Alpine fell alive into the hands of the enemy.

Lieutenant Frascoli did not stay there even dead: while the Battalion retreated fighting, his orderly Domenico Caspani, an Alpine from Sondrio, saw the officer fall dead and went back towards the advancing Soviets to take him away. He took the inanimate body on his shoulder and ran to rejoin his companions; but the Soviets were about to catch up with him, and then the Alpino Caspani laid the officer's body on the ground, turned towards the riflemen and began firing, stopping them for a moment; then the lieutenant charged up again and ran off. Still the Soviets, another sota, another magazine fired, and away again; and again and again and twice and thrice, until Caspani could lay his dead lieutenant between our lines and wipe his bloody face and put him back together for the last time.

In the summer of 1942 the Soviets attacked the Italian lines near the Don river's banks in what the Italians called the First defensive battle of the Don, routing the *Sforzesca* Division (nicknamed by the Soviets *Tchikay divizijon*, Run away Division). Despite the reaction of the 3rd

Celere and the Black Shirts of the *Tagliamento* Group, the Red Army had managed to pass the Don with twenty- seven Battalions of the 197th and 203rd RifleDDivisions and the 14th Guards Division, which led to a retreat of the Italian line on positions by Jagodny and Tchebotarewskij despite the strenuous resistance of the Black Shirts. of the *Tagliamento* Group certified on Tchebotarewskij's hill 232.2.

On 25th September the 14th *Guards* conquered the stronghold of Tchebotarewskij held by the *Tagliamento* Group and the remains of the 1st / 54th (less than a thousand men in all) and the Italian line seemed on the point of collapsing even at Jagodny on the 28th, but when the hill 187.9, garrisoned by the XXV Bersaglieri, was about *to* fall into the hands of three Soviet Regiments (610th / 20rd div., 619th / 203rd, 889th / 197th); a violent counterattack by the *Alpini* Skiers of the *Cervino* re-established the situation, and the Soviets retreated without making other attempts against Jagodny. The day after the intervention of 11. Panzer-Division put an end to the Soviet offensive.

In Jagodny the Alpini had to deal for the first time with the multiple rocket launchers RS-132 *Katjusha*, which, apart from the first psychological impact, did not particularly impress the *Cervinotti*: Lieutenant Vicentini recalls that

> Once they sent us running to replace a *Bersaglieri* Battalion in Jagodnyj, in the area where Izbushensky's charge took place. Arrived, we got into position and there I saw the katiushes for the first time. It felt like the end of the world.
>
> What power do the *Katjushas* have? From the stories it seems to be a psychological weapon, which tends to disorient with its noise rather than having a devastating power in terms of impact with the ground. Meanwhile, it is a weapon against infantry that has no demolition power.
>
> The missiles are cylinders of about one meter, half are propellant and the rest are explosive. When it hits the ground it explodes and makes a lot of noise, a huge blaze comes out, a single rocket contains a quantity of explosives twenty times that of a 75 grenade. It is impressive when it arrives: the light trails sail overhead with a deafening noise, phenomenal. Then over time you learn to know and get used to them too
>
> ... They are very inaccurate, they cover the space of a hundred meters of territory.
>
> Usually it's a dozen shots even if some people talk about twenty-four shots, but that's all lies.
>
> Establishing the number, however, should not be difficult, it would be enough to count the locations, the tracks mounted on the trucks from which they are launched.
>
> Like we had batteries, the ones I saw (in the form of wrecks during the advance and in operation, when I was captured) had a precise number of weapons, they took six trucks and with them they launched the *Katjushas*.
>
> These had the great advantage that, being placed on a truck, after firing the shots they moved quickly a hundred meters and did not suffer the counter battery.
>
> (...) However, mortar bombs were more dangerous [the Soviets used heavy mortars from 120mm ndA] ... were more precise.
>
> The splinters were bigger. While the artillery shell penetrates the ground, so the explosion cone is less open, it is more vertical, the mortar shell tears apart as soon as it touches the ground and when you throw yourself into it you have to stay glued to the ground and hope to be as far as possible from the explosion so as not to be hit by the splinters.

About the battle, it is also worth mentioning the testimony of the *Alpino* Bartolomei of the 80th AA Company:

> We were in front of Bahmutkin.
>
> There was a Soviet attack and a subsequent furious counterattack by the 3rd Bersaglieri Regiment. We were able to see the various stages of the battle.
>
> Then we too advanced on the *Cervino*, participating in the fight.
>
> The Russians began to withdraw, thanks to the contribution of our mortars, and retreated on a new line that was 250-300 meters from the point where they had started to conquer the altitude defended by the 3rd *Bersaglieri* Regiment of the *Celere* Division.
>
> The battle was very hard. We managed to repel the opponent who left several dead on the ground.
>
> A gruesome sight: mangled bodies, severed feet still in shoes. For the first time I was witnessing the horrifying spectacle of real war …
>
> Some of the Soviet deads wore - over theirs - the summer uniform of the Italian infantry: as they advanced, the Soviet units had seized the warehouses of the *Sforzesca* Division and disguised themselves to deceive us.
>
> In the following days - due to the heat - the unburied bodies began to stink in such a way that the smell prevailed over that of our ration. So Captain Lamberti ordered them to be buried.
>
> We then dedicated ourselves to fortifying the new defense line with trenches, small bunkers and lookout posts, obtained at the cost of hard work of pick and shovel. The Soviets were doing the same thing, reinforcing their front line.

Summarizing the evolution of the battle, in the very first days the Soviet units managed to put the Italian units in serious difficulty, and there was no lack of episodes of subsidence and panic phenomena among the departments, especially in the ranks of the 2nd *Sforzesca* Infantry Division. Later, with the influx of reserves, the Italian units fought well and managed to contain the enemy advance, even without being able to regain all the lost positions.

Overall, however, these operations highlighted the precariousness of the Italian positions on the river and the loss of the position to the south of the same, and from one of these bridgeheads on the front held by the Axis, as we will see later, it left in the following month in December the *Malij Saturn* operation which would have determined the total defeat of the Romanian Divisions and of the 8th Italian Army on the Don front.

The battle caused a serious crisis in relations between Italians and Germans due to the initial serious defeat of the *Sforzesca* Division and the phenomena of disintegration of some departments of this Division.

The result was a significant loss of mutual trust and *brotherhood of arms* between the two Axis Powers.

The even more serious thing for the Italian arms was the departure of General Messe, the best officer available to the Supreme Command. He was deeply irritated by the German behavior and in strong contrast with General Gariboldi, newly appointed commander of the 8th Army, asked for and obtained the recall to his homeland and therefore left the command of the XXXV Army Corps.

Mussolini himself recognized in his book *Storia di un anno* that *it was a mistake* not to leave General Messe in command of the ARM.I.R[2]. and Galeazzo Ciano insinuated in his *Diary* that the Chief of Staff himself, Marshal Ugo Cavallero, did not like too much the possible designation of Messe due to the popularity he enjoyed both in the ranks of the Army and in the country itself.

The German Command will try to settle the disagreements and, worried about the stability of the Don sector, sent General Kurt von Tippelskirch with full powers of supervision and control as German liaison officer with the 8th Army.

Tippelskirch had been appointed on August 27, German liaison officer, replacing a major, in the hope that a general officer could have more influence on the Italian command, while seeking to create a governing body capable of act autonomously in critical situations.

Faced with the precariousness of the tactical situation in the Serafimovič bridgehead, the command of the *Heeresgruppe B* decided to launch on September 1st in the direction of Kotovksij, a combined counterattack of German formations and the *Vestone* and *Valchiese* Battalions, supported by two L6 light tanks platoons.

The poorly coordinated attack was overall a failure and the four rifle Divisions deployed by the Soviets retained their valuable positions in the greatly expanded bridgehead between Yagodny and Bolshoi.

In conclusion, the Soviets were unable to obtain territorial advantages, but the conquest of altitude 220 in the bend of Verchnij Mamon provided them with a valid launch base; just as, on the far right of the line, they had forced the allied troops to abandon the right bank of the Don and assume a new and particularly vulnerable alignment.

In the First Defensive Battle of the Don, the 8th Italian Army had to suffer heavy losses; 2,704 dead and missing and 4,212 wounded, considering the period between 20th August and 1st September 1942.

From that date the clashes ceased and almost nothing happened on the front until November 19th, 1942, the day on which the Soviets launched the Operations *Uranus* and *Saturn*, the great counter-offensives in the Stalingrad sector.

On 12th September 1942, in Moscow, Stalin received Marshals Zukhov and Vassiliewsky, returning from an inspection from the Stalingrad front.

Stalin asked them to study how to avoid the fall of the city, and the two generals, the next day, presented their plans: a pincer offensive on the flanks of the 6th Armee, in the sectors held by the Romanian troops. Stalin agreed.

Zhukhov had the task of preparing the northern part of the offensive, and Vassiliewsky the southern one.

---

2 *Armata Italiana in Russia*, Italian Army in Russia (the 8th Army)

During the planning work, Zukhov realized how, thanks to the reservations made available by the information about the non-aggressive attitude of the Japanese in Manchuria, the Red Army could have dealt the decisive blow against the Germans and their allies.

Zukhov was convinced that the *Heeresgruppe Mitte* could be annihilated, and presented his ideas to Stalin, who approved them, entrusting him with preparing the offensives in collaboration with Vassiliewsky.

Conventionally, such offensives were given names of Roman gods. The offensive against Stalingrad would be called *Uranus*.

The *South West* and *Don Fronts*[3] would attack to the north, and, the next day, the Stalingrad Front would also attack from the south, aiming at the annihilation of the Romanian 3rd Army (Gen. P. Dumitrescu) and 4th Army (Gen. C. Costantinescu).

The pincer would close near Kalach, encircling Paulus and his 6. *Armee*.

If *Uranus* had succeeded as planned, Operation *Saturn* would have been unleashed against the Italian 8th Army, which would have had Rostov as its ultimate goal, the destruction of *Heeresgruppe B* and the isolation of Heeresgruppe A in the Caucasus. At one hundred, Zhukhov planned Operation *Mars*: the *Western Front* and *Kalinin Front* would annihilate the Rjev salient, held by the 9. *Armee*.

If the offensive had been successful, the Western Front would have started Operation *Jupiter* against *Heeresgruppe Mitte* in the Vyazma region. Mars was supposed to start before *Uranus*, but this was prevented by weather conditions, so when the Soviets attacked, they noticed that the German reserves had been moved towards Stalingrad, and Zukhov decided to extend the offensive in the Velikie Luki sector with a motorized Corps, and, in case of favorable developments, to point on Smolensk, destroying the entire *Heeresgruppe Mitte*. Zhukhov then managed to persuade Stalin to leave the 2nd Guard Army, northwest of Voronez, at his disposal, in anticipation of *Jupiter*, rather than assign it to *Saturn*.

The operation was renamed *Malyï Saturn*, *Little Saturn*, because the operational plan was downsized when Vassiliewsky was forced to request the *emergency* dispatch of the 2nd Guard Army to counter von Manstein and his Wintergewitter offensive.

The new goal would have been the annihilation of Italian 8th Army. and German *Heeresgruppe Don*, an objective only partially achieved.

It has often been argued that *Uranus* concentrated 60% of the Soviet forces. This is not true. The *South West*, *Don* and *Stalingrad Fronts* made up 20% of the Red Army forces (1,103,000 men, 1,560 tanks, 928 aircraft and 15,501 guns), while the forces destined for *Uranus* and *Jupiter*, the *Kalinin* and the *West Fronts* and the defensive region of Moscow, constituted 35% of total (1,890,000 men, 3,375 tanks, 1,175 aircraft and 24,682 guns).

Soviet actions against the Italians started mainly from the bridgeheads that the enemy had created on the right bank of the river.

---

[3] A Soviet Front corresponded to a German Heeresgruppe.

The Italian 8th Army. had a cordon deployment on a front extended for 270 kilometers, without depth and without an adequate density of troops, and without reservations: although Gariboldi had repeatedly pointed out the situation to *Heeresgruppe* B (von Weichs) it had never been paid attention.

After the First Defensive Battle of the Don in August, the Soviets remained in possession of two bridgeheads on the western bank of the Don: on the front of the II Corps the salient of Verch Mamon, the largest, and a smaller one in the sector of XXXV, the Ogalew loop, known to Italians as the Phrygian cap loop due to the shape of the river bank.

Meanwhile, at the beginning of October the *Monte Cervino* Battalion had been aggregated to the Headquarters of the Alpine Army Corps in Rossosch as Army reserve. When the Soviets unleashed the *Malyï Saturn* offensive in December, the Skiers of the *Cervino* were again sent to the front line to support the *L'Aquila* Battalion of the 9th *Alpini* Regiment of *Julia* Alpine Division engaged in the battle of Ivanovka, on December 22, for possession of the important road junction of Seleni Yar; during that clash the Alpine Skiers, with individual assaults, knock out several Soviet T-34 tanks with clusters of hand grenades, incendiary bottles and anti-tank mines.

The Soviets, with infantry and T34 tanks, managed to encircle the *Cervino* and *L'Aquila*; to get the Italians off the hook some German assault guns intervened in support.

Lieutenant Sacchi shouting *Cervino! Pista!* took off his skis and jumped on a German *Sturmgeschütz* III, already in the midst of the Soviet troops: all the *Alpini* imitated him, and on every Stug.III a group of Skiers in white overalls went up, firing volleys, throwing bombs, dispersing the enemy infantry and gaining the admiration of the Germanic gunners. The survivors of *Monte Cervino* (the 80th AA company withdrew separately, rejoining the Battalion on December 31st) reached Rossosch on December 30th.

 At this point, we have to spend few words about the bad relations between *Alpini* and German soldiers, so much emphasized by antifascist authors such as Revelli and Rigoni Stern for reasons that are anything but honest, in a sort of anti-German victimization, to justify theItalian turncoat of September 1943.

About the increasingly tense relation between the two Armies we can quote the *Monte Cervino*'s Second Lieutenant Vicentini:

> The 52nd German [Regiment] withdrew with us.
>
> Our Battalion commander [Lieutenant Colonel. D'Adda, ndA] told me that he should have had orders from the II Corps and, since he was not there, he would have made himself available to the Germans.
>
> But the Germans immediately started playing carrion. They told us to occupy a certain position in front of Ivanovka, but soon after we realized that the Germans were no longer on our side, they had gone away leaving us alone.
>
> They had withdrawn the troops, the infantry, keeping the artillery in the rearmost position. My commander at that point, seeing that I spoke German, took me as an interpreter and took me with him.

We went to an *isba* where there was the German war council.

Entering the *isba* he said *"I am the commander of the Italian Battalion, you have given me the order to occupy the quotas. Why did you withdraw and tell me nothing?"*

They prevaricated but my commander took off the German iron cross from his neck, the one with the laurels [this is prob. of the *Kriegsverdienstkreuz*, not of the *Ritterkreuz* ndA], which is worth our silver medal, and slammed it on the table saying: *"I don't know what to do with your medal if you then treat me in this way."*

There was the famous general Eibl who, afterwards, collaborated a lot with us. If you weren't loud with the Germans, you weren't respected.

Such unfriendly acts between the two Axis allies occurred not infrequently during the retreat.

If the lack of camaraderie of the Germans is often emphasized by Italian memoirs, there was no lack of completely similar cases that saw the Germans as victims

On 31st December 1942, the *Cervino* Skiers threw themselves against the advancing T34 tanks, setting them on fire with Molotov cocktails, throwing their hand grenades in bunches, hitting the tracks with all their weapons.

Corporal Angelo Gabrieli, an mountainman from Rocca Pietore, commanded an anti-tank gun: when the Soviets tanks attacked, Gabrieli was wounded, but continued to fire against the advancing tanks: a T34 was hit and immobilized, while the other tanks turned back.

Gabrieli did not move in anticipation of a foreseeable new Soviet offensive attempt; he ordered the servants to leave and was left alone, with the piece pointed.

When the attack resumed, one of the T34s headed towards him. Gabrieli waited, to hit him in the tracks, to have him near; he let the T34 advance further, until it was a few meters away, then fired.

The shot hit the T34 to a track, but the tank, too close to the shooter, by force of inertia did a few more meters turning on itself, and Corporal Gabrieli was crushed with his piece under the wagon, from which he came out with his hands raise the crew that surrendered. On 15 January the Soviets reached Rossosch, defended by the *Monte Cervino* and the XXX *Guastatori Alpini* (Alpine Assault Engineers) btg; a column of fifteen T34 tanks bypassed the lines and managed to penetrate the hamlet of Rossosch, were was the HQ of the Italian Alpine Army Corps; *Monte Cervino* Battalion together with the *Guastatori Alpini*, fighting between the houses managed to contain the assault with anti-tank mines, incendiary bottles, destroying almost all the tanks; in the following days the attacks of the Soviet armored troops inflicted heavy losses on the *Cervino* which had to retreat.

Units started to fall back after Soviet renowed tank attacks on 14–15th January 1943, with the *Monte Cervino* Bn acting as rearguard. The last to withdraw westwards, the battalion split up; some *Alpini* were carried on lorries, others on sleds, but the majority – about 120 men – marched on foot after abandoning their skis. The first two groups, mainly the wounded and the 80th Cp AA, managed to escape encirclement, but the rest of the battalion struggled against attacks by both Soviet armour and partisans, and finally were either killed or captured. Out of the 226 Alpini who were listed missing; only 15 men were ever to return from the Soviet POW camps.

Alpino Bartolomei still remembers:

It was rumored that the *Monte Cervino* Battalion would soon be back in line, but it was not necessary to leave, because at dawn on January 15th, 1943, the Soviet tanks reached Rossoš.

The general alarm went off for all the troops that were in the city. We settled in the points where the passage of the armored vehicles was expected. To face them we had hand grenades, muskets and a single 47/32 anti-tank gun, whose caliber was unfortunately ineffective on thicker armor.

There was a sound of strafing coming from the railway station area.

Our patrol, having moved to a path at the back of some isbas, heard the rattling of Russian wagons heading for the Kalitva river: they were certainly intent on crossing the frozen stream and then heading to the station. So we too, with caution, went to Kalitva.

On reaching it, we saw a Soviet tank half-sunk, the turret hatch was open. We of the 1st Company decided to track down the adversaries who, for sure, were hiding in the surrounding isbas.

Divided into patrols, we searched the area. A patrol entered an isba: the women inside ensured they were alone. Nobody believed their words, and with good reason. Two opposing soldiers were discovered, who opened fire. Two *Monte Cervino's Alpini* were injured, but the Soviets had the worst. During the retreat from Rossosch the *Cervino* fought as a rear guard, against the Soviet regulars and the Partisans who infested the rear of the front.

On January 22nd, 1943, the seventy-five surviving Alpini of the *Monte Cervino* Battalion engaged in the last fight, trying to clear the way towards the Axis lines. The Alpini attacked at the cry of *Pista!* managing to break through the Soviet encirclement and get out of the pocket; the remains of the *Cervino*, with the green pennant, insignia of the Battalion, managed to save themselves by reaching Karkhov.

The *Monte Cervino* Battalion, the only one among the Battalions of the Italian Royal Army, received the Golden Medal, usually granted to the Regiments: officers and soldiers were decorated with two Golden medals, 35 of Silver and 54 of Bronze, mostly to memory, as well as 65 War Merit Crosses and an unspecified number of German *Eisenkreuz*.

Out of 564 men, 114 fell in combat, 226 were missing. only 15 returned from Soviet captivity.

Ninety percent of the officers fell on the field.

The bravery of the *Cervinotti* is summarized in the motivation of the Golden medal for Military Bravery granted to the Battalion:

> Battalion of Alpine Skiers, cast in a granite block of energy and alpine daring, in twelve months of Russian campaign has given uninterrupted proofs of exceptional bravery and unparalleled spirit of sacrifice.
>
> Unwavering in its defense, impetuous and overwhelming in its offense, it has always achieved the goals indicated to him.
>
> In the great Russian winter offensive it wrote shining pages of glory.
>
> It is the first to support the impetus of massive infantry masses supported by armored units that have overwhelmed the resistance of the Front, contains them with an active and daring defense, nails them to the ground until reinforcements arrive that allow him a truce after a fight of two weeks completed without stopping, without shelter, in exceptionally adverse weather conditions.

Surrounded by a far superior number of infantry and armored vehicles, although reduced to a few survivors mostly wounded, frozen and exhausted, it sustains a desperate struggle and with the bravery of all its men and the sacrifice of many, it manages to break the circle of iron and fire.

Afterwards it continues to march in the endless snowy plain, overcomes all the obstacles that stand in his way, rejects the enemy who pursues it, and, haggard, reaches the allied lines in an aura of victory equal to that of the most high Alpine traditions of history.

(Olkawactka - hill 176 - Klinowiy - Jahodnj - Iwanowka - hill 204 - Kolkos Selenj Iar - Rossosch - Olkawactka, Russia, February 1942 - February 1943).

Also Soviet sources must record that

Among the riflemen there were heavy losses.

There were 236 soldiers and officers killed, while many more were wounded - but no precise order was kept of them. During the fighting, the commander of the 86th Regiment himself, Alexei Andrianovich Zaiijkin, was mortally wounded, [and] was awarded the Order of Lenin.

It must be remembered how the Soviet units were fully staffed, equipped with automatic armament and perfectly equipped for the winter, as well as being motorized and supported by tanks and aviation, unlike the Alpini, on foot, absolutely understaffed for losses, without adequate anti-tank and anti-aircraft armament, but still combative and capable of inflicting heavy losses on the opponent.

Here a consideration must be made: despite the heavy losses, the positive result of the *Monte Cervino* Battalion, and in general of the Alpine Army Corps is due to the fact that, although trained for mountain combat, the *Alpini* were the most suitable Italian soldiers. fighting at those temperatures and moving in the snow in such adverse atmospheric conditions, especially the men of the Cervino, particularly specialized in acting and fighting in extreme climatic situations; moreover, unlike those forced to travel long distances on foot in the steppe, the men of *Monte Cervino* used skis, thus speeding up the movement: the much criticized a posteriori dislocation of the Alpine troops in the Don plain turned out to be all other than improvising; and also the Romanian *Vanatori de Munte* and the German *Gebirgsjäger* were also employed in the steppe just like the *Alpini*.

In 1943 what remained of *Monte Cervino* returned in Italy; the reconstituted Battalion was assigned to the XX *Raggruppamento Sciatori Alpini*, part of the Italian 4th Army with occupation duties in France; at the time of the Italian armistice of September 1943 the Battalion was captured by the Germans, with the exception of the 80th AA company; part of the men joined Mussolini's Italian Social Republic while others made the opposite choice, joining the *Resistance*.

▲ The "cervinotti" to the assault of Soviet infantrymen under artillery fire.

▲ *Pista!*

▲ ▼ The Alpini on the assault under Soviet fire.

▲ Alpini under enemy fire.

▼ The Alpini attackers throw themselves into a "balka". Note the Breda 30 machine gun and the servant with the ammunition box.

▲ The Alpini reach the abandoned enemy positions.

▼ Soviet positions are raked.

▲ ▼ A Breda machine gun mod.37 in action.

▲ The Soviet lines seen from the position of the "Matterhorn".

▼ Alpine gunners in the steppe, summer 1942. The difference also in the clothing with the Matterhorn is very evident. (Courtesy of the National Historical Alpine Museum).

▲ ▼ Mortar Alpinists of the 80th company AA.

▲ Detail of the previous photo. Note the dagger from Ardito supplied to the battalion for close combat.

▲ Alpini with 81 mm mortar. Note the frieze with the Alpine eagle and the regimental number.

▼ Servants with 81mm mortar.

▲ A Mortar Alpinist regulates the raising of the cane.

▼ Adjusting the mortar for aiming.

▲ The 81 mm mortar ready to fire...

▼ Mortars open fire on Soviet positions.

▲ ▼ Battalion Matterhorn mortar men dismantle the mortars after the action.

▲ ▼ Matterhorn Alpines on the edge of a Balka.

▲ Camouflaged snipers lurking in ambush. The Alpini were excellent riflemen, often poachers accustomed to high mountain hunting and long-term stakeouts.

▼ Matterhorn patrol with Breda 30 machine gun.

MONTE CERVINO TODAY

After the war, on 1st September 1952 the 1st Platoon *Alpini Paracadutisti* (Mountain Paratroopers) *Tridentina* was established for the need to reconstitute, within the Alpine Troops, a department with a high specialized connotation able to move in the mountain environment, also adding the ability to operate in the third dimension. For this reason, the staff was trained at the Viterbo Parachuting Center to obtain the parachutist license.

The following year, similar platoons were set up under the *Julia* and *Taurinense* brigades and, in 1956, also in *Orobica* and *Cadore*, thus reaching 5 platoons for 5 Alpine brigades.

On April 1st, 1964, the Alpine Paratroopers Company was set up, employed by the 4th Alpine Army Corps. The personnel of the dissolved Alpine paratroop platoons of the five Alpine Brigades converged within the Company. The Alpini Paratroopers Company of the 4th Army Corps continued its specialized path in this way, training and qualifying its personnel both in the mountain environment (skiing and rock) and in parachuting.

On 1st January 1990 the Parachute Alpini Company was renamed *Monte Cervino* thus inheriting the glorious traditions of courage and military prowess of *Monte Cervino* Ski Battalion.

In 1995 the Company was transferred to the *Vittorio Veneto* barracks in Bolzano

On July 14th, 1996, the Italian Army General Staff in a framework of reorganization of the Armed Force and by virtue of the brilliant results obtained by the Alpine Paratroopers elevated the Company to the rank of Battalion..

In 2000 the *Monte Cervino* Battalion became a FOS unit (Forces for Special Operations), after having received the *Ranger* qualification, that is light infantry unit particularly trained and specialized in providing support to unconventional operations such as direct actions, raids, ambushes, etc. ., in a non-permissive environment.

The 4th "*Ranger*" Alpine Paratrooper Regiment is a Department of Army Special Forces capable of planning, organizing and conducting the entire spectrum of Special Operations.

So direct actions, special reconnaissance and military assistance, with a particular aptitude for conducting direct actions ensuring a high level of specialization in combat in the mountain and arctic environment.

In the context of what are the Army Special Forces, the 4th Regiment is the one most specialized in use in the mountains; so much so that the preparation and training part in the specific environment has a substantial impact and relevance.

Not only is the aspect of mobility taken care of, but also the ability to use, for example, skiing, as a movement tool in a snowy environment for the conduct of direct military action.

Direct action is an offensive action that is based on some principles that we can summarize as: surprise factor, mass and firepower.

This is one of the differences that exist between the 4th Ranger Alpine Parachute Regiment and the other Special Forces Regiments. Rangers operate on a minimum platoon basis (mass principle); a platoon with high numerical consistency while the other Special Forces units are based on detachments (numerically reduced unit).

From all this the aptitude for conducting direct actions. The Special Forces Department is assigned the achievement of a strategic objective that has direct implications in what is the military campaign. To do this, special equipment, materials, armaments and types of insertion are used, as well as personnel specifically equipped, selected, trained and prepared to conduct that specific activity.

The Ranger Battalion today consists of three companies:

1st Company *Satanas bjieli* (*White devils*: the nickname given to *Cervinotti* by the Soviets)

2nd Company *Angeli Neri* (Black Angels)

80th Company *Lupi della Steppa* (*Wolves of Steppe*). The Company takes the name and number of the 80th Company AA employed in Russia

The men of the 4th Ranger Alpine Parachute Regiment are present in the most important operational theaters with different tasks:

In **Italy** they are employed as *Joint Rapid Responce Forces* (JRRF). In particular, the JRRF represents a pool of existing high and very high operational readiness inter-force capacity / assets, from which to draw to ensure a rapid response to national and multinational needs.

Lebanon, **Somalia**, **Libya** and **Afghanistan**: the 4th Alpine Parachute Regiment is providing the *Close Protection Team* (CPT) to the Mission Commanders.

In **Niger**, on the other hand, the Regimental operators have recently changed hands after having "*opened*" the theater.

Lebanon: Employment is in the training and training of Lebanese Armed Forces personnel; Ranger operators have developed a Sniping Course in the mountain area for operators of the Lebanese Special Forces

Antarctica: personnel employed in support of the ENEA Mission.

Iraq: Support for the Iraqi Police Forces.

Afghanistan: The Special Operations Task Group, based on the 4th Ranger Alpine Parachute Regiment, has followed the partner units of the Afghan Special Security Forces in the conduct of training activities throughout the entire training course.

Serbia: support for the NATO mission.

Today the 4th Regiment motto is *Mai strack* (*Never tired*)

▲ ▼ The Alpini observe the opposing positions overflown by the Luftwaffe.

▲ ▼ After the defeat of the Soviet offensive in August 1942, Italian flametrowers clean up the bush on the banks of the Don from the last Soviet infiltrators.

▲ Soviet T 34/76 tank destroyed by Italian anti-tank guns.

▼ A captured T34 tank.

▲ An Italian soldier observes an abandoned T34. The red flag signals the possible presence of mines.

▼ A 47/32 gun of the 80th company.

▲ Monte Cervino's mortarman in the Don steppe.

▼ Alpini in the Don steppe, autumn 1942.

▲ Alpini advance in the rasputiza, the mud that made Soviet roads impassable.

▼ 80th Company AA's Mortarmen apposted near an isba, autumn 1942.

▲ The capture of Soviet soldiers.

▼ Column of trucks headed for the Don.

▲ General Italo Gariboldi, commander of the 8th Italian Army, delivers the rewards for military bravery for the fighting in the summer of 1942.
On the stage you can see the commander D'Adda (with the Alpine cap).

▲ Summer of 1942. General Gariboldi decorates the fighters of the Russian front. On the right, captain Giuseppe Lamberti of Cervino decorated with his second Silver medal.

▼ Monte Cervino's men during the same ceremony. Note the white hemp equipment.

▲ Detail of Captain Lamberti. Note the Assaul troops' dagger.
After the war Lamberti was disbarred from the Italian Army for collaborating with the Soviets after he fell prisoner.

▲ Monte Cervino 47/32 anti-tank gun crew in action (courtesy of the Museo Na-zionale Storico degli Alpini)

▼ Alpini in their lodgings at the Don (courtesy of the Museo Nazionale Storico degli Alpini)

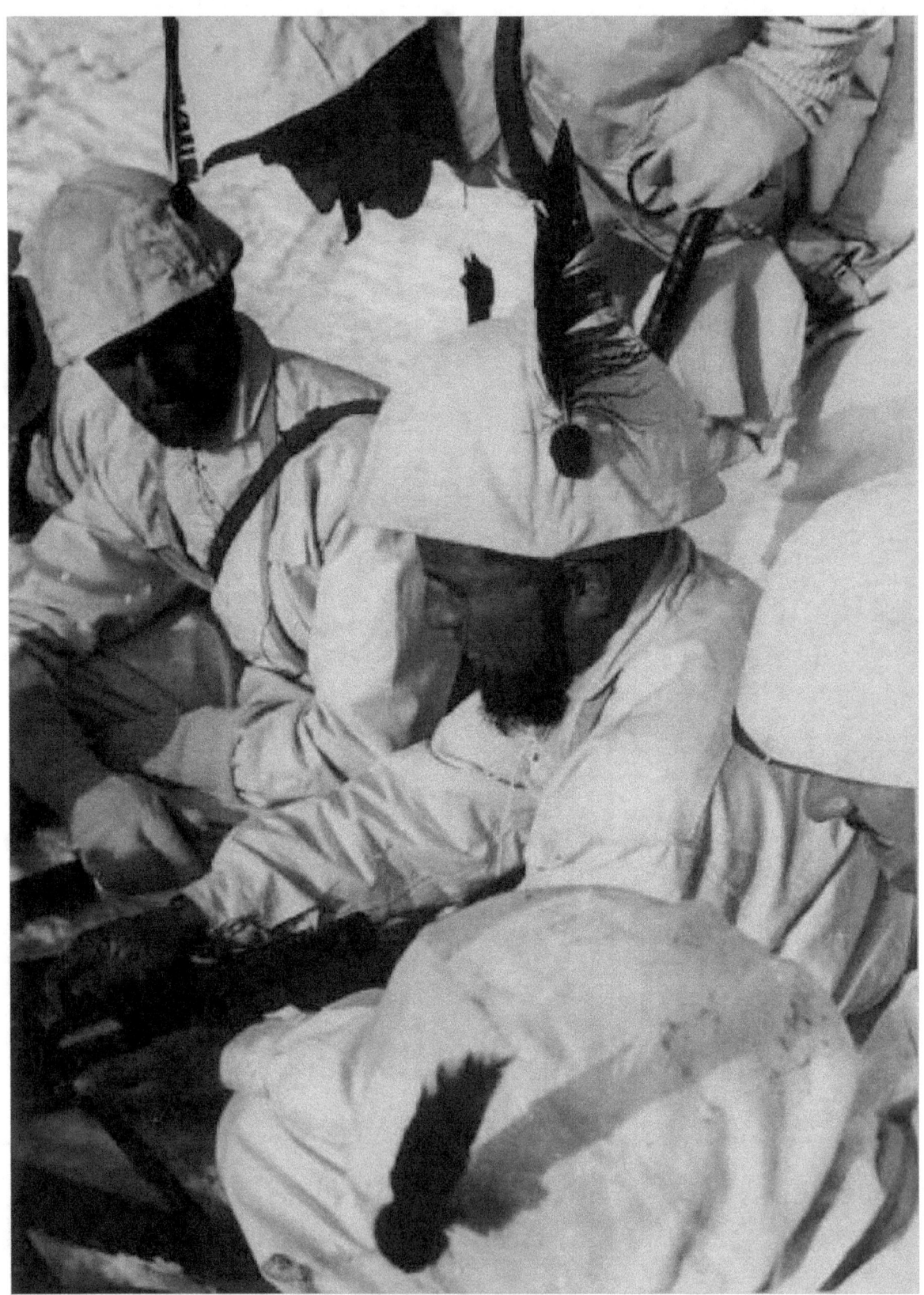
▲ Unit of Monte Cervino in withe camo suit, winter of 1942. The Alpini are armed with the excellent MAB 38 submachine guns.

▲ Alpine skier in sentry duty, wearing padded wool gloves. On his feet he wears a pair of padded 'valenky'.

▲ An Alpine skier dons padded boots called 'valenky' by the Russians before going out on patrol.

▲ A Cervino's patrol holds a briefing with its officer before the action.

▼ The patrol in the snowy steppe.

▲ ▼ Alpini fasten their skis before a reconnaissance.

▲ 47/32 mm guns from the 80th AA company in position in the snow.

▼ 47/32 mm gun of the 80th AA company.

▲ ▼ Skiers in action.

▲ ▼ Captain Lamberti in Russia, 1942. The photo is usually published inverted, with the tassel and the feather on the right (below), probably due to the fact that Lamberti was left-handed.

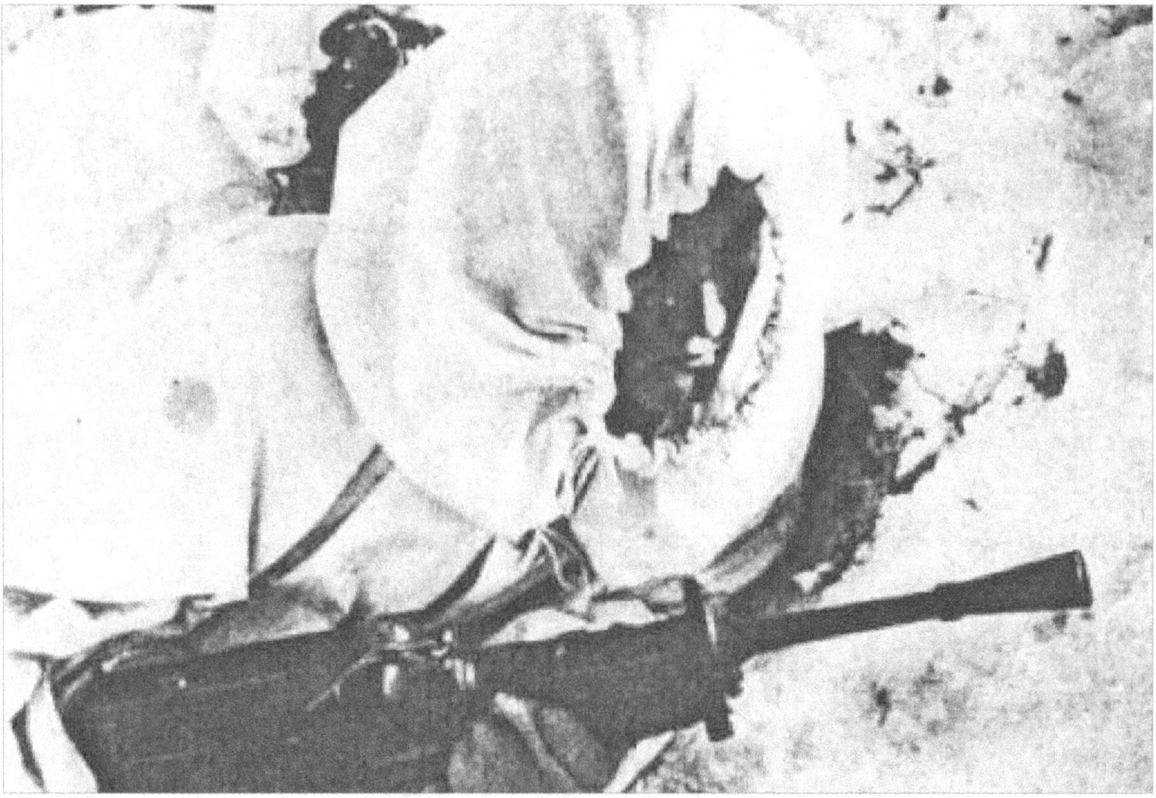

▲ December 1942 Explorer of the Monte Cervino Btg, armed with a Breda 30 machine gun.

▼ A Monte Cervino ski patrol in a birch forest on the banks of the Don.

▲ Second Lieutenant Carlo Vicentini near a Breda 30 machine gun, a weapon that tended to freeze at low temperatures.

▼ A patrol in the Don river sector in the winter of 1942. The Alpini are armed with 91/38 TS musket and MAB 38 submachine guns.

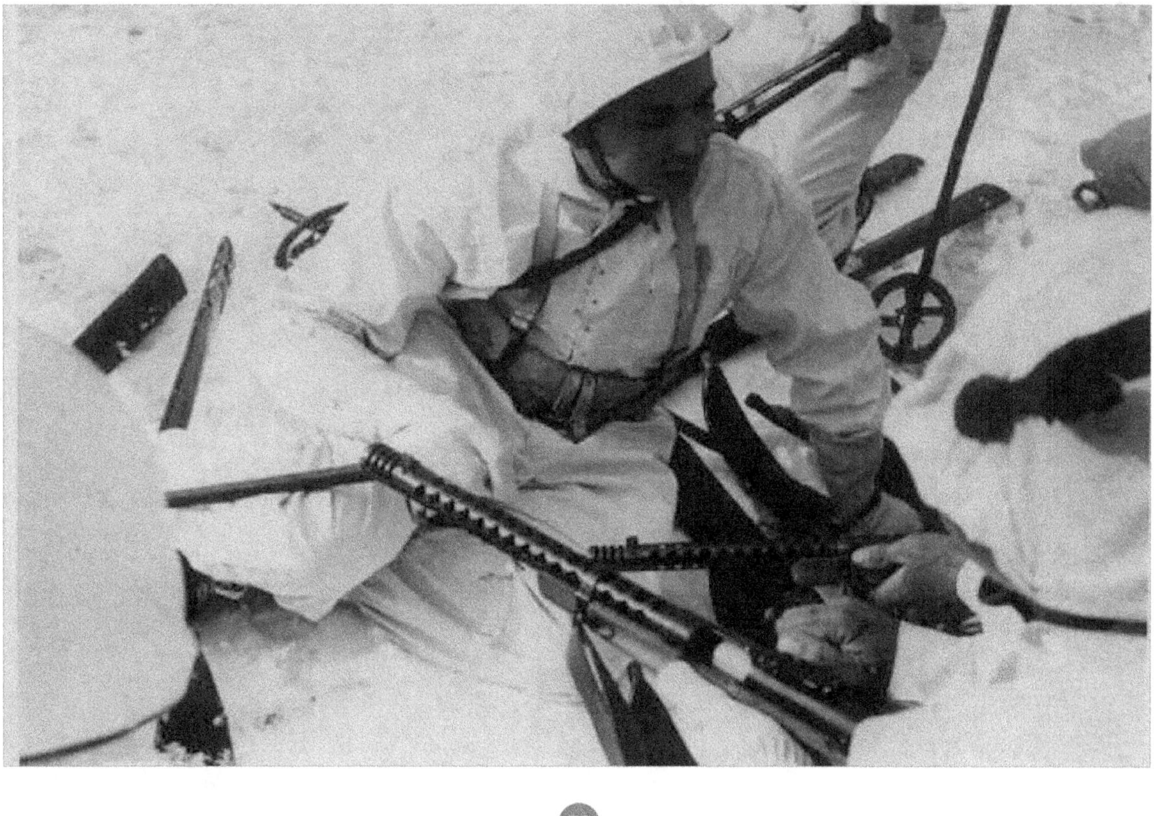

▲ Alpini on the front line near the banks of the Don.

▼ Cervino's Alpini on reconnaissance.

▲ A Cervino's NCO with camouflage gear. balaclava and white wool gloves, ano-rak, white cloths and linen.

▼ A Cervino's patrol with a litter mounted on skis.

▲ Skiers armed with MAB 38 SMG.

▲ A patrol of the Monte Cervino with two Italian infantrymen inlight gray-green wool overcoat, December 1942.

▼ Detail of the previous photo. The abysmal difference in equipment is clearly evident.

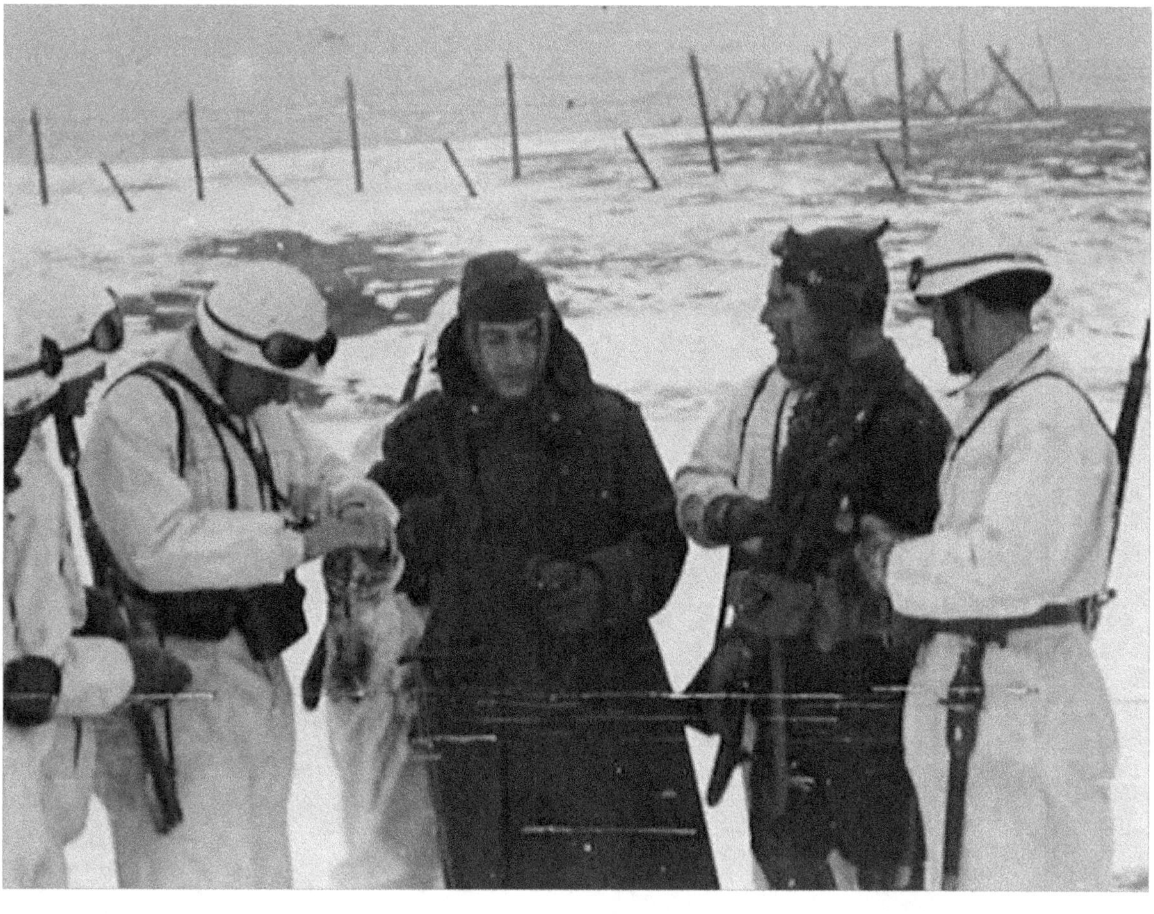

▲ A moment of rest for a lunch in the snow...

▼ Cervino's Alpini in action, December 1942.

▲ An officier of Monte Cervino observes the Orthodox cathedral of Rossosch, headquarters of the HQ of the Italian Alpine Army Corps.

▲ Alpini del Cervino in reconnaissance.

▼ Alpini del Btg Monte Cervino, report in our lines the body of Lieutenant Carlo Sacchi, Commander of the 1st CompanyRussia Kolkoz Selenyi Jar, December 1942.

▲ The retreat of the Alpine Army Corps near Arbusowo, January 1943.

▼ The long column of Italian soldiers in retreat, January 1943.

▲ The medical Second lieutenant Enrico Reginato (Treviso, 5th February 1913 - Padua, 16th April 1990), awarded with Golden Medal for Military Bravery. Reginato remained in Soviet concentration camps for twelve years because he refused to adhere to the communist ideology, during which time he put his medical knowledge at the service of fellow prisoners of various nationalities, especially Germans and Romanians, and was subsequently decorated by the governments of the Republic German Federal and Romanian Republic, after Ceaucescu's fall. Returning to Italy he continued to serve in the Army, concluding his career as Major General.

▲ Ivanovka's fights on the cover of La Tribuna Illustrata magazine The Alpini of Monte Cervino Btg climb into German tanks (really assault gus) to attack the Soviet rifles at close range.

▲ Postcard of the Monte Cervino battalion with the motto *Pista!*

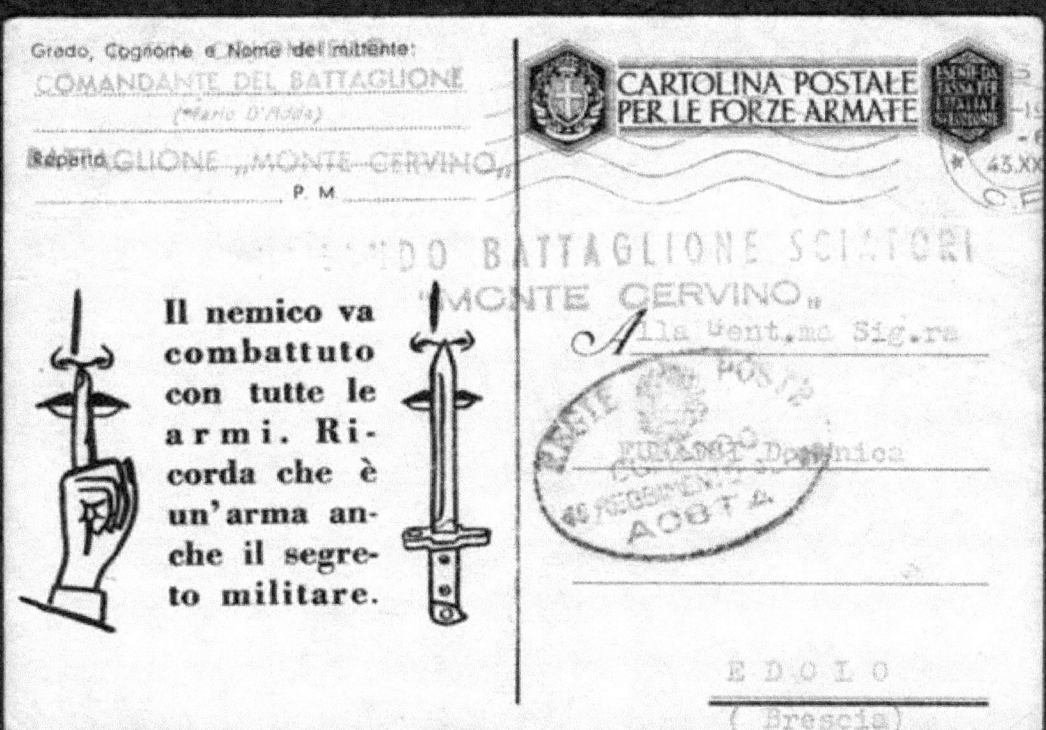

▲ Free postcard sent by Commander D'Adda to the mother of an Alpine soldier missing in Russia on June 2nd, 1943.

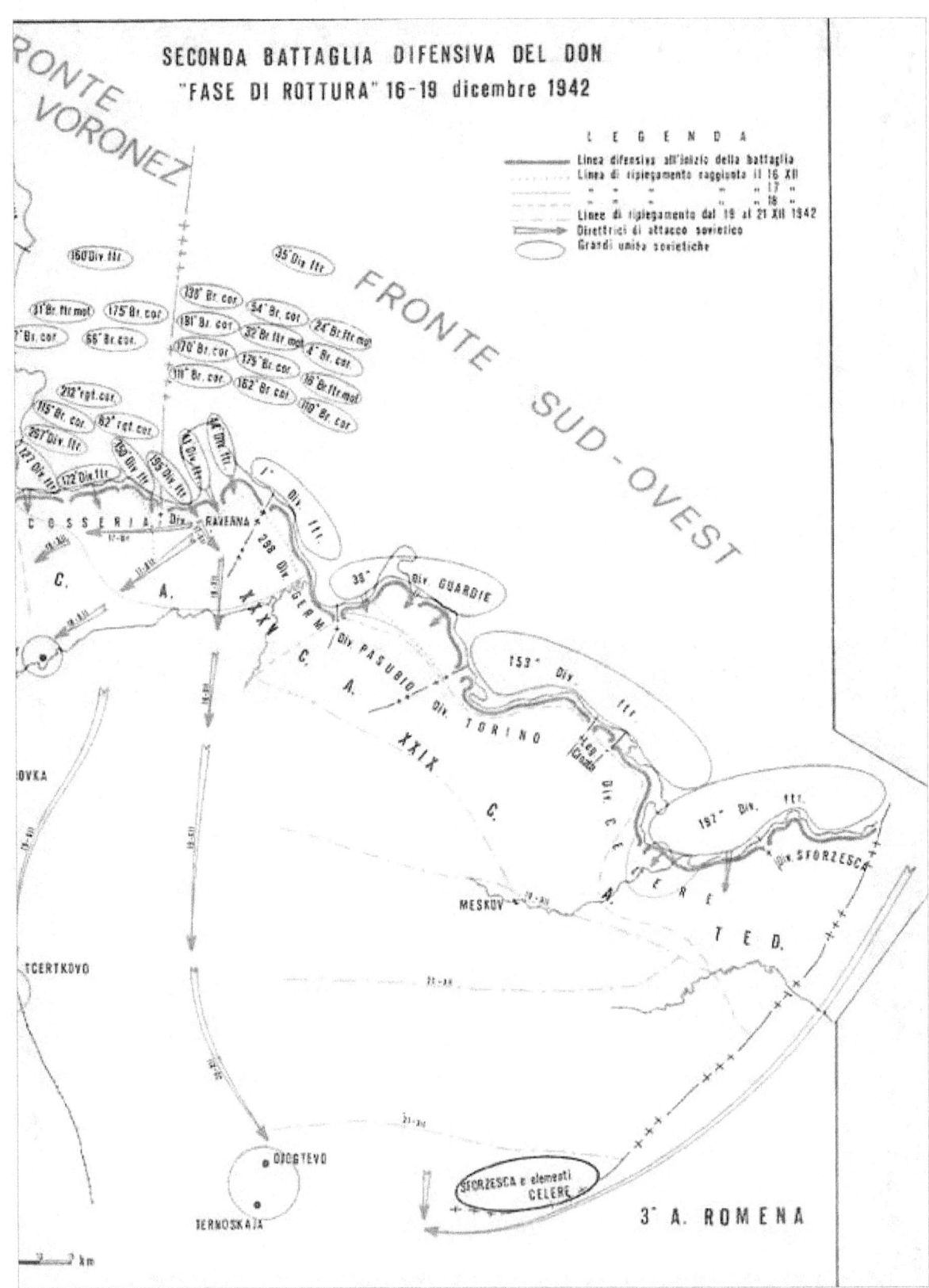

▲ Operation Malij Saturn, Little Saturn.

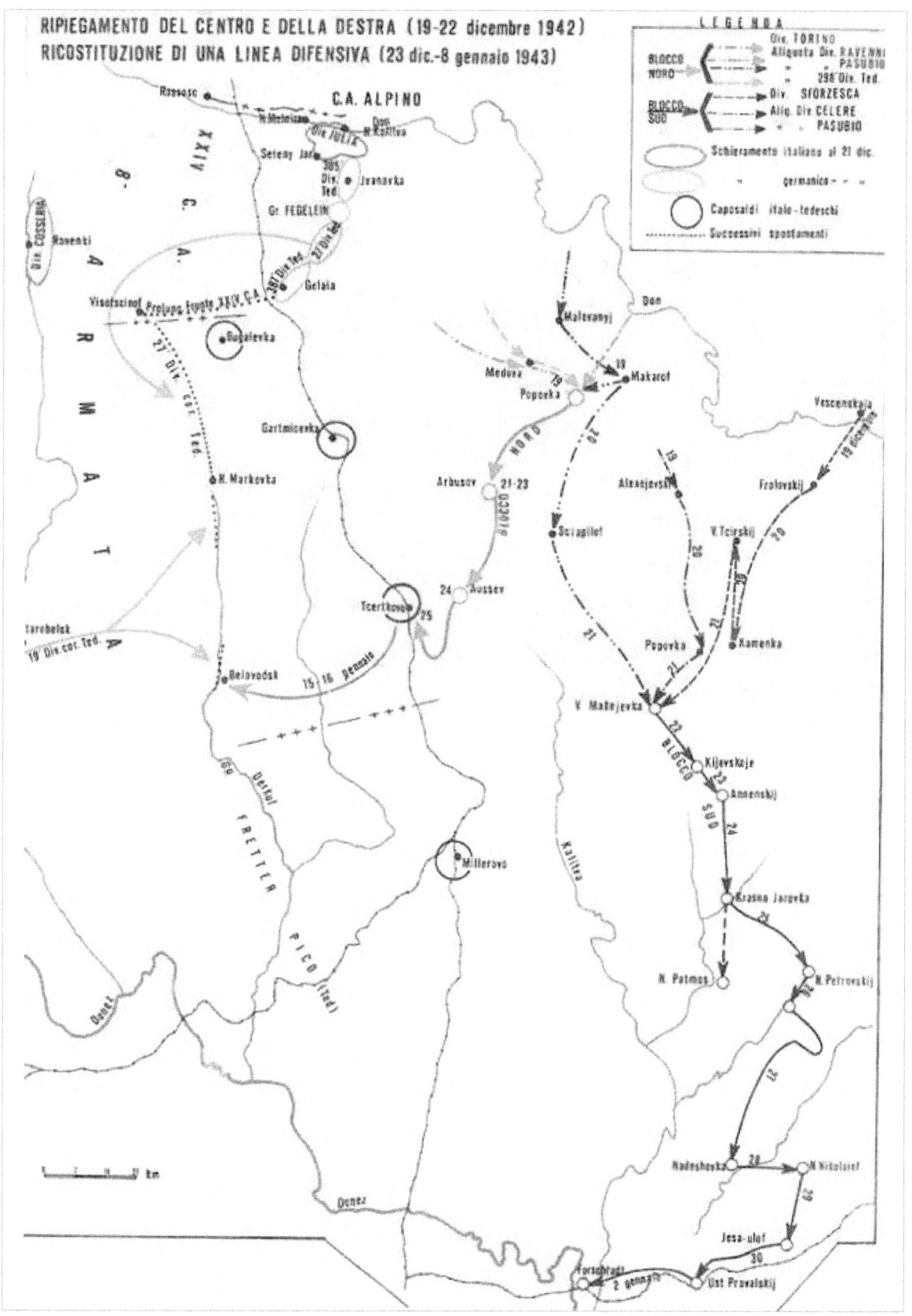

▲ A column of Axis prisoners, January 1943. Only 14% of Italian prisoners survived imprisonment in the Soviet camps of Stalin.

DECORATED OF THE BATTALION SKIERS BATTALION MONTE CERVINO, 1942-1943

Decoration	M	Rank	Surname	Name
MOVM		Tenente medico	REGINATO	Enrico
MOVM	M	caporale	GABRIELI	Angelo
MAVM		Tenente Colonnello	D'ADDA	Mario
MAVM		Tenente Colonnello	D'ADDA	Mario
MAVM		Capitano	LAMBERTI	Giuseppe
MAVM		Capitano	LAMBERTI	Giuseppe
MAVM		Capitano	MERLINI	Enrico
MAVM	M	Tenente	CORTE DI MONTONARO	L.
MAVM		Tenente	SACCHI	Carlo
MAVM	M	Tenente	SACCHI	Carlo
MAVM	M	Sottotenente	FRASCOLI	Vitaliano
MAVM		Sottotenente medico	LINCIO	Domenico
MAVM		Sottotenente	ROMANIN	Gino
MAVM		sergente maggiore	ANDREONI	Aldo
MAVM	M	sergente maggiore	FABBRI	Guido
MAVM	M	sergente	CHIANALE	Renato
MAVM		sergente	DELLA MEA	Adolfo
MAVM		caporal maggiore	BRONDELLO	Antonio
MAVM		caporal maggiore	DE GIORGI	Enrico
MAVM		caporal maggiore	MARTIN	Pietro
MAVM		caporal maggiore	MIUZZI	Antonio
MAVM		caporal maggiore	SOLA	Severino
MAVM		caporale	CASTELLI	Bruno
MAVM		caporale	FUMAGALLI	Primo
MAVM		caporale	IPPOLITI	G.Battista
MAVM		caporale	QUATTRINI	Battista
MAVM		alpino	ARTUS	Giovanni
MAVM		alpino	BERTON	Guido
MAVM		alpino	CASPANI	Domenico
MAVM		alpino	FRIGERIO	Salvatore
MAVM		alpino	LOCATELLI	Attilio
MAVM		alpino	MINO	Raimondo
MAVM		alpino	MONTI	Oberdan
MAVM		alpino	MORA	Angelo
MAVM		alpino	RIBUL	Ugo
MAVM		alpino	ROSA'	Celeste
MAVM		alpino	TAVCAR	Virgilio
MBVM		Capitano medico	BIANCHI	Giovanni
MBVM		Capitano	BORDONE	Mario
MBVM		Tenente	BAISI	Giuseppe
MBVM	M	Tenente	CARBONI	Livio
MBVM		Tenente cappellano	CASAGRANDE	Attilio
MBVM		Tenente cappellano	CASAGRANDE	Attilio
MBVM		Tenente	CASTELLANI	Gastone
MBVM		Tenente	CORTE DI MONTONARO	L
MBVM		Tenente	NOCENTE	Luigi
MBVM		Sottotenente	CARUSO	Francesco
MBVM		Sottotenente	DURIGON	Lido
MBVM		Sottotenente	GRIGATO	Luigi
MBVM		Sottotenente medico	LINCIO	Domenico
MBVM		Sottotenente medico	LINCIO	Domenico
MBVM		Sottotenente	MARINI	Gianpiero
MBVM		Sottotenente	MODIGLIANI	Giuseppe
MBVM		Sottotenente	TOSANA	Emanuele
MBVM		Sottotenente	VICENTINI	Carlo
MBVM		Sottotenente	VICENTINI	Carlo
MBVM		aiutante di battaglia	VIVIANI	Tarcisio
MBVM		sergente maggiore	AONDIO	Pietro
MBVM		sergente maggiore	BERNASCONI	Gian Elia
MBVM		sergente maggiore	JORDANEY	Romano
MBVM		sergente	CAVALLER	Umberto
MBVM		sergente	DELLA BELLA	Luigi
MBVM		sergente	INVERNIZZI	Massimo
MBVM		sergente	INVERNIZZI	Massimo
MBVM	M	caporal maggiore	AROBBIO	Eligio
MBVM		caporale	CASTELLUCCI	Vincenzo
MBVM		caporale	DEMANEGA	Bruno
MBVM		caporale	SCAIOLI	Nicola
MBVM		alpino	AUDIBERT	Giuseppe
MBVM		alpino	BAGNIS	Giuseppe
MBVM		alpino	BASSI	Pierino
MBVM		alpino	BERTOZZO	Ermenegildo
MBVM		alpino	BRUGNETTI	Giuseppe
MBVM		alpino	BRUN	Angelo
MBVM		alpino	CACCIALUPI	Bruno
MBVM		alpino	COLOMBO	Emilio
MBVM		alpino	DAGANI	Pasqualino
MBVM		alpino	DAMOLI	Luigi

MBVM		alpino	DANIELE	Benedetto
MBVM		alpino	DEL GRANDE	Casimiro
MBVM		alpino	FAROVINI	Carlo
MBVM		alpino	FRIGERIO	Salvatore
MBVM		alpino	LANCINI	Amerigo
MBVM		alpino	LAZZARI	Marino
MBVM	M	alpino	MORATTI	Battista
MBVM		alpino	OLIVERO	Matteo
MBVM		alpino	PERONO	Giacomo
MBVM		alpino	SOLA	Severino
MBVM		alpino	TOMERA	Giacomo
MBVM		alpino	USSEGLIO NANOT	Aldo
MBVM		alpino	VIALE	Giovanni
CGVM		Capitano	BIASI	Egidio
CGVM		Tenente medico	BIANCHI	Giovanni
CGVM	M	Sottotenente	AUDINO	Francesco
CGVM		Sottotenente	CARUSO	Francesco
CGVM		Sottotenente	SNICHELOTTO	Francesco
CGVM		aiutante di battaglia	VIVIANI	Tarcisio
CGVM		sergente maggiore	ANTONIETTI	Cesare
CGVM		sergente maggiore	BRUNA	Stefano
CGVM		sergente maggiore	CRESPI	Gianfranco
CGVM		sergente maggiore	FALETIC	Ludovico
CGVM		sergente maggiore	GIORDANETTO	Andrea
CGVM		sergente maggiore	MAINARDIS	Vito
CGVM		sergente maggiore	MARCUCCI	Tullio
CGVM		sergente maggiore	MIUZZI	Antonio
CGVM		sergente maggiore	PAGGI	Guerrino
CGVM		sergente maggiore	PIATTO	Aldo
CGVM		sergente	ABENI	Palmiro
CGVM		sergente	ANTONIETTI	Cesare
CGVM		sergente	CROCI	Mario
CGVM		sergente	GAMBIRASI	Pietro
CGVM		sergente	GOBBO	Antonio
CGVM		caporal maggiore	BAGNIS	Edoardo
CGVM		caporal maggiore	BONETTI	Antonio
CGVM		caporal maggiore	COGLIATI	Raffaele
CGVM		caporal maggiore	LOSS	Gustavo
CGVM		caporal maggiore	MABELLINI	Italo
CGVM		caporal maggiore	MAGGIORI	Cesare
CGVM	M	caporal maggiore	PETENZI	Antonio
CGVM		caporal maggiore	ROSSIO	Francesco
CGVM		caporale	NEMO	Mario
CGVM		caporale	PARNISARI	Giovanni
CGVM		alpino	BACCANELLI	Alfredo
CGVM		alpino	BIANCO	Domenico
CGVM		alpino	BOSETTI	Paolo
CGVM		alpino	CAPPELLETTI	Ercole
CGVM		alpino	CASTAGNA	Lino
CGVM		alpino	CATULLI	Antonio
CGVM		alpino	CAUDA	Venerio
CGVM		alpino	CHARLIN	Alberto
CGVM		alpino	CHATALIN	Stefano
CGVM		alpino	CORDERO	Antonio
CGVM		alpino	CORTICELLI	Leonardo
CGVM		alpino	DALMASSO	Spirito
CGVM		alpino	DANIELE	Benedetto
CGVM	M	alpino	DE MARIA	Giuseppe
CGVM		alpino	GALLI	Pietro
CGVM		alpino	GARREU	Francesco
CGVM		alpino	GROSSI	Piero
CGVM		alpino	JUGLAIR	Tobia
CGVM		alpino	MALPELI	Nello
CGVM		alpino	MIGLIORE	Costanzo
CGVM		alpino	MINO	Raimondo
CGVM		alpino	MONDINELLI	Pietro
CGVM		alpino	PACCHIOTTI	Aldo
CGVM		alpino	RAZA	Antonio
CGVM		alpino	ROSA'	Celeste
CGVM		alpino	SALVADORI	Ferdinando
CGVM		alpino	SARZETTI	Antonio
CGVM		alpino	SPILLER	Renato
CGVM		alpino	STEFANI	Giuseppe
CGVM		alpino	THONELET	Ambrogio
CGVM		alpino	TONOLA	Leopoldo
CGVM		alpino	TRABUCCHI	Patrizio
CGVM		alpino	VALLORSI	Alfredo

BIBLIOGRAPHY

D. Agasso 1958, "Gli sciatori della morte", *Storia illustrata*, Anno II n°2.

P.P. Battistelli, P. Crociani 2011, *Italian Army Elite Units & Special Forces 1940-43*, Oxford.

G. Bedeschi 2005, *Fronte russo c'ero anch'io*, 2 voll., Milano

O. Bovio 1999, *In alto la bandiera. Storia del Regio Esercito*, Foggia

F. Bigazzi, E. Žirnov 2002, *Gli ultimi 28. La storia incredibile dei prigionieri italiani dimenticati in Russia*, Milano

F. Cappellano 2002, "Scarpe di cartone e divise di tela..." Gli stereotipi e la realtà sugli equipaggiamenti delle truppe italiane in Russia durante la Seconda guerra Mondiale, "Storia militare" n°10.

A. Ceol (cur.) 2009, *Il battaglione Alpini sciatori "Monte Cervino". La voce dei superstiti*, Aosta

R. Cossaro 1984, *Il battaglione sciatori "Monte Cervino" sul fronte greco-albanese*, Milano

P. Crociani, P. Battistelli 2011, *Italian Army Elite Units & Special Forces*, Oxford

E. Faldella 1959, *L'Italia nella seconda guerra mondiale. Revisione di giudizi*, Bologna

Gruppo Medaglie d'Oro al Valor Militare 1965-1973, *Le Medaglie d'Oro al Valor Militare*, I-III, Roma

P. Jowett 2000, *The Italian Army 1940-1945 [1] Europe 1940-43*, Oxford

P. Jowett 2006, *The Italian Army at War. Europe 1940-43*, Honk Kong.

L. E. Longo 1991, *I "Reparti speciali" italiani nella Seconda Guerra Mondiale 1940-1943*, Milano

A. Massignani 1991, *Alpini e Tedeschi sul Don*, Valdagno

E. Reginato 1955, *12 anni di prigionia nell'URSS*, Milano

A. Ricchezza 1972, *Storia illustrata di tutta la Campagna di Russia*, Milano

O. Ricchi, L. Striuli 2007, *Fronte Russo. C.S.I.R. Operations 1941-1942*, Virginia Beach

E. von Rintelen 1947, *Mussolini l'alleato*, Roma

P. Romeo di Colloredo 2010, *Croce di Ghiaccio. CSIR e ARMIR in Russia, 1941-1943*, Genova

P. Romeo di Colloredo 2019, "*Pista!* Il battaglione Alpini sciatori "Monte Cervino", 1941-1943", *Ritterkreuz*, n. 66, Novembre 2019

G. Scotoni 2007, *L'Armata Rossa e la disfatta italiana*, Trento

T. Schlemmer 2005, *Die Italiener an der Ostfront 1942/1943. Dokumente zu Mussolinis krieg gegen die Sowjetunion*, München-Berlin (tr. It. Roma-Bari 2009)

C. Tomaselli 1943, *Battaglia sul Don*, Milano-Roma

Ufficio Storico dello Stato Maggiore dell'Esercito 1946, *L'8a Armata italiana nella Seconda battaglia difensiva del Don (11 gennaio 1942- 31 gennaio 1943)*, Roma

Ufficio Storico dello Stato Maggiore dell'Esercito 1948, *Le operazioni del C.S.I.R. e dell'Armir dal giugno 1941 all'ottobre 1942*, Roma

Ufficio Storico dello Stato Maggiore dell'Esercito 1978, *L'Italia nella Relazione Ufficiale Sovietica sulla Seconda Guerra Mondiale*, Roma

Ufficio Storico dello Stato Maggiore dell'Esercito 2000, *Le operazioni delle Unità italiane al Fronte russo*, IVa ed, Roma

L. Vaglica 2006, *I prigionieri di guerra italiani in URSS. Tra propaganda e rieducazione politica :"L'Alba" 1943-1946*, Milano 2006

F. Valori 1967, *Gli italiani in Russia. La Campagna del C.S.I.R. e dell'ARMIR*, Milano

B. Vandano 1964, *I disperati del Don. La battaglia del Don 1942- 1943*, Milano

L. Viazzi 1984, *1940- 1943 I diavoli bianchi. Gli Alpini sciatori nella Seconda guerra mondiale. Storia del battaglione "Monte Cervino"*, Milano.

A. Werth 1964, *Russia at War 1941-45*, New York

R. Zizzo 1996, *1942-1943. La tragedia dell'ARM.I.R. nella Campagna di Russia*, Campobassovolta giunti in Italia.

TITOLI GIÀ PUBBLICATI
TITLES ALREADY PUBLISHING

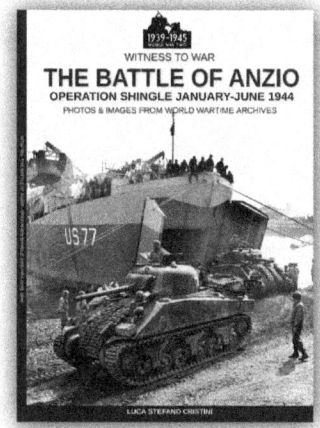

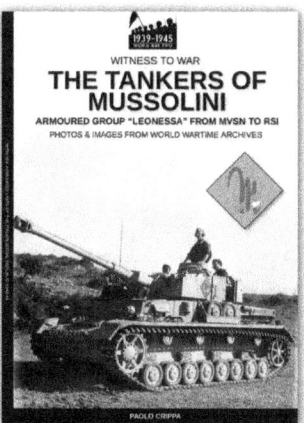
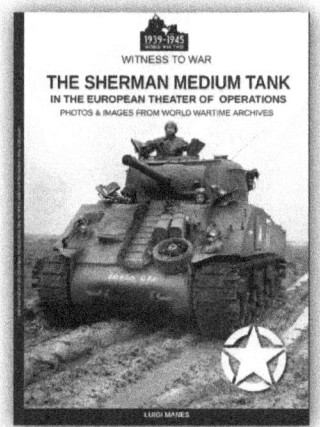

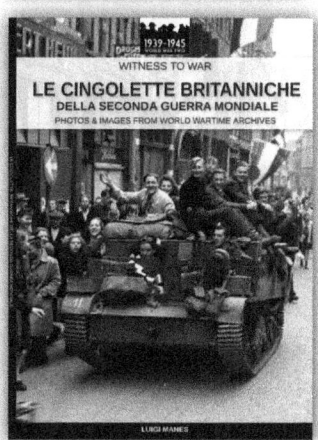

www.ingramcontent.com/pod-product-compliance
Lightning Source LLC
LaVergne TN
LVHW081545070526
838199LV00057B/3784